Avila v. Nita City Hospital

Avila v. Nita City Hospital

Gwen R. Stern
Drexel University
Kline School of Law

Andrew J. Stern
Kline & Specter PC

Philip Pasquarello

NITA®
National Institute for Trial Advocacy

Address inquiries to:

Reprint Permission
National Institute for Trial Advocacy
1685 38th Street, Suite 200
Boulder, CO 80301-2735
Phone: (800) 225-6482
Fax: (720) 890-7069
Email: permissions@nita.org

ISBN 978-1-60156-755-0
eISBN 978-1-60156-756-7
FBA 1755

Printed in the United States of America

ASPEN PUBLISHING

Official co-publisher of NITA.
aspenpublishing.com/NITA

Contents

A Note from the Authors

This brief note provides some background information and additional instruction on how to best utilize this unique NITA case file. Although the names and witnesses have been changed, the depicted events are based on an actual case that was litigated and tried by Andrew J. Stern as lead counsel. The detailed fact pattern and supporting illustrative exhibits provide law students and trial lawyers with an opportunity to creatively and effectively argue their themes and theories. *Avila v. Nita City Hospital* can be applied to teach trial advocacy techniques on liability and/or damages and includes an ample supply of expert witnesses. The liability and damage phase each contains its own witnesses and exhibits to facilitate bifurcation or to allow trial as one matter. In sum, our goal was to create a case file that teaches realistic trial advocacy techniques to students, but would also challenge trial lawyers who seek the thrill of perfecting their craft by trying this fascinating case.

We suggest that the reader review the jury instructions and verdict forms as a good starting point to learn medical malpractice law in the state of Nita.

Have fun!

ACKNOWLEDGEMENTS

The authors would like to thank Donna Duggan, legal assistant to Gwen Stern, for her tireless assistance in helping to put this case file together. Thank you, also, to Facebook and Twitter for permission to use likenesses of their sites. We are also especially thankful to our outstanding NITA editor, Virginia Judd, Esq. for her guidance, creativity, precision, and her excellent editing comments.

Case Summary

This is a medical malpractice case file based on a real case tried by co-author Andy Stern in November of 2015 in Philadelphia, PA. The case file revolves around the alleged delay in diagnosis and treatment of severe bacterial infection/bacterial meningitis of a two-year-old boy that resulted in permanent, profound sensorineural hearing loss. The case involves a three-day illness that culminated in an eight-hour visit to the emergency room from March 11, YR-2 starting at 9:00 p.m. until the diagnosis at 4:30 a.m. on March 12, YR-2.

Specifically, the plaintiff-mother Shirley Avila first noted that her two-year-old son Timothy "Timmy" Avila presented fever and cold-like symptom starting on March 8, YR-2. She consulted with the hospital's telephonic nurse on the morning of March 9, YR-2, who instructed her to take the toddler to the Nita City Hospital Emergency Department (ED) if the symptoms worsened. On March 10, Shirley made an early visit to the ED because Timmy's fever persisted at 104F. They were sent home after three hours because Timmy's fever went down and he appeared to be displaying simple cold-like symptoms.

On the evening of March 11 YR-2, Shirley summoned an ambulance to take Timmy back to the ED. By this time, Timmy had a three-day history of 104F fever, cough, runny nose, reduced oral intake, reduced urinary output, irritability, decreased activity, inconsolability at times, and was now presenting with increased work of breathing, tachycardia, and tachypnea. The treating ED nurse Jamie Miller, RN and attending physician Dr. Casey Smith evaluated Timmy and treated Timmy's condition as a viral respiratory disease, a common occurrence with this group of complaints. The doctor ordered a chest x-ray, which came back as normal. The medical providers' plan was to just monitor Timmy in the ED for viral respiratory illness. The doctor ordered Tylenol for Timmy's fever and a nebulizer treatment for his reported wheezing, which was in addition to the nebulizer treatment he received in the ambulance. At this point, Timmy appeared to be doing better. The medical providers continued to monitor him without further testing or treatment, despite the mother's claim that Timmy had become lethargic. At 4:15 a.m., Timmy started to complain of neck pain. Treating nurse Jamie Miller, RN, evaluated him and then called in Dr. Smith. At 4:30 a.m., Dr. Smith came in to evaluate Timmy. The boy's eyes were starting to cross. Dr. Smith immediately ordered a lumbar puncture and blood work, and it was performed promptly thereafter. The results of the blood work were returned by 5:00 a.m. The blood work revealed a grossly abnormal white blood cell count and an elevated C–reactive protein level. The lumbar puncture revealed that Timmy had bacterial meningitis. The plaintiffs claim that had the nurse and the doctor properly evaluated Timmy earlier for a bacterial infection, he would have been admitted for further evaluation, testing, and antibiotic therapy, and this would have prevented the progression of his significant bacteremia to bacterial meningitis, thereby avoiding the permanent injuries he has sustained.

The defense responds that the nurse and the doctor reasonably assumed that Timmy's signs and symptoms were consistent with a viral upper respiratory infection/bronchiolitis, which improved with the nebulizer treatment in the ambulance. His signs and symptoms appeared to improve in the hospital prior to the complaints of neck pain and crossed eyes. The defense maintains that they acted as quickly as possible to diagnose his bacterial meningitis once Timmy had complained of neck pain, a symptom commonly associated with bacterial meningitis. Further, they maintain that even if antibiotics had been given earlier, it would not have changed the outcome in the short span of time at issue.

Case Summary

Special Instructions for Use as a Full Trial

1) The plaintiff and the defendant must call at least two witnesses listed as that party's witnesses on the witness list.

2) Except for Shirley and Jules Avila, all witnesses are written to be gender and race neutral. They may be played by a person of any gender or ethnic background.

3) All witnesses called to testify who have identified the parties, other individuals, or tangible evidence in statements or prior deposition testimony must, if asked, identify the same at trial. Additionally, witnesses have knowledge of all documents on which their signatures appear.

4) Each witness who testified previously agreed under oath at the outset of his or her testimony to give a full and complete description of all material events that occurred and to correct the transcript of such testimony for inaccuracies and completeness before signing the deposition transcript.

5) All exhibits in the case file are authentic. In addition, each exhibit contained in the file is the original of that document unless otherwise noted on the exhibit or as established by the evidence.

6) All signatures are authentic. No advocate may attempt to impeach a witness by arguing that a signature on a transcript, statement, or exhibit does not comport with a signature or initials on an exhibit.

7) Other than what is supplied in the problem itself, there is nothing exceptional or unusual about the background information of any of the witnesses that would bolster or detract from his or her credibility.

8) The case file is a "closed universe" of facts, and advocates may use only the materials in the file except that participants may look up unfamiliar medical terms.

9) "Beyond the record" shall not be entertained as an objection. Rather, advocates shall use cross-examination to impeach the witness regarding any material facts not contained in the case file. Where asked, witnesses must admit that the fact to which they have testified is not in their statement or testimony.

10) The Statement of the Case shall not be used as evidence or for examination or cross-examination of any witness.

Procedural Matters

11) Federal Rules of Evidence and Federal Rules of Civil Procedure apply.

12) If the defendant is found liable, an evaluation of the damages may take place before the jury or on a separate date, depending on the decision of the instructor.

13) All dispositive pretrial motions have been filed and denied; no further dispositive motions (other than optional Motions in Limine and Motions for Judgment as a Matter of Law) will be entertained.

14) It is stipulated that all experts reviewed all expert submissions provided by the parties and they must testify within the fair scope of their reports and curriculum vitae.

Other Instructions

15) All years in these materials are stated in the following form:

   a) YR-0 indicates the actual year in which the case is being tried (i.e., the present year);

   b) YR-1 indicates the next preceding year (please use the actual year);

   c) YR-2 indicates the second preceding year (please use the actual year), etc.

16) Electronic exhibits can be found at the following website:

http://bit.ly/1P20Jea
Password: Avila1

STIPULATIONS

1) Timmy Avila has a normal life expectancy.

2) All exhibits have been authenticated to be admissible at trial, but any other evidentiary objection is permitted.

3) Timmy's hearing was tested at the time of his birth and was normal.

4) Bacterial meningitis was the cause of Timmy Avila's hearing loss.

5) Timmy Avila's past medical expenses relating to his time at Nita City Hospital on March 11 and March 12, YR-2, as well as any subsequent visits to Nita City Hospital, amounts to $35,000.

6) The parties stipulate that in the damages portion of this trial, damages for plaintiff's a) pain and suffering, b) lost wages, c) past medical expenses, and d) future medical expenses are the only monetary damages that the plaintiff seeks. Damages for any other reasons are not at issue in this case.

7) All parties and witnesses are of at least of normal intelligence and none has or ever has had a mental condition that would impact a person's perception, memory, or ability to respond to questions on cross-examination.

8) Shirley Avila called the Nita City Hospital help line on March 9, 2012, and spoke with a nurse, who advised her to give Timmy Tylenol and monitor him. There are no negligence allegations with regard to this call.

9) Timmy Avila was seen at the Nita City Hospital emergency department on March 10, presenting with a 104F fever, stuffy nose, and irritability. Timmy was released after three hours, when a dose of Tylenol reduced his fever, on the assumption that he had a simple cold. There are no negligence allegations with regard to this decision.

10) Throughout his visit to the Nita City Hospital emergency department on March 11 and March 12, YR-2, Timmy Avila's vital signs (temperature, heart rate, blood pressure, and respiratory rate) were abnormal.

11) Once Timmy Avila was diagnosed with bacterial meningitis at 5:30 a.m. on March 12, YR-2, the appropriate antibiotics were administered. There is no dispute regarding the appropriateness of the type of dosage of antibiotic administered.

12) The normal resting heart rate for a child of two years is 80–130 beats per minute, and the normal respiration rate for a child of two years is 25–30 breaths per minute.

Witness List

PLAINTIFF:

1. Shirley Avila
2. Jules Avila
3. Sam Simmons
4. Jody Holt
5. Ryan Donnelly
6. Cameron Patrick

DEFENDANT:

1. Jamie Miller
2. Casey Smith
3. Logan Lewis
4. Elliott Green
5. Andy Biddle
6. Chase Myers

Except the mother and grandmother, witnesses are gender neutral and may be either male or female.

IN THE DARROW COUNTY
COURT OF COMMON PLEAS

SHIRLEY AVILA, AS PARENT AND NATURAL GUARDIAN ON BEHALF OF HER MINOR SON, TIMOTHY AVILA,	:	**COMPLAINT**
	:	**THIS IS NOT AN ARBITRATION**
Plaintiffs	:	**JURY TRIAL DEMANDED**
v.	:	Case No. 17-108
NITA CITY HOSPITAL, Defendant	:	

CIVIL ACTION—MEDICAL PROFESSIONAL LIABILITY ACTION

I. SUMMARY OF THE CASE

1. This is a professional medical malpractice liability case against defendant Nita City Hospital and its agents and/or employees for the catastrophic and permanent injuries sustained by the minor plaintiff Timmy Avila.

II. VENUE

2. This Court has proper venue, because the medical malpractice that is the subject of this Complaint occurred in Nita City, Nita, at Nita City Hospital.

III. THE PARTIES

3. Minor Plaintiff Timmy Avila was born on January 8, YR-4, and was two years old at the time of the medical malpractice in question. Timmy is a citizen of Nita and resides with his mother, Shirley Avila, at 2215 Market St., Nita City, Nita.

4. Defendant Nita City Hospital is a Nita corporation and medical health care facility, organized and existing under the laws of the state of Nita, and created for the purpose of diagnosing, treating, and directing appropriate care to patients such as Timmy Avila. At all times relevant to this case, defendant had its principal place of business located at 1100 Chestnut St., Nita City, Nita.

5. At all times relevant to this case, the following healthcare providers were employees of Nita City Hospital and were acting as actual agents on behalf of defendant Nita City Hospital:

    a. Jamie Miller, RN

    b. Casey Smith, MD

6. At all relevant times relating to the treatment in question, a healthcare provider–patient relationship existed between Timmy Avila and Nita City Hospital, along with the other agents and/or employees of Nita City Hospital, and will be the subject of discovery. Plaintiffs are asserting professional liability claims against this defendant, as well as all agents and/or employees of defendant, as referred to in this complaint.

IV. OPERATIVE FACTS IN SUPPORT OF PROFESSIONAL LIABILITY CLAIM

7. On March 11, YR-2, plaintiff mother Shirley Avila called Nita City emergency services because of the deteriorating condition of her son, Timmy. After evaluation and a nebulizer treatment by the EMS crew, Timmy was taken by ambulance, along with his mother, to the emergency department of the Nita City Hospital. At that time, Timmy had already been seen at the emergency department on March 10, YR-2, complaining of a two-day fever and cold-like symptoms, including runny nose, cough, reduced oral intake, decreased activity, decreased urine output, irritability, and inconsolability. By the time of the March 11, YR-2 visit, Timmy had complained a total of three days of those symptoms and now additionally presented with wheezing, elevated heart rate, and increased work of breathing.

8. At the time of Timmy's presentation on March 11, YR-2, the attending physician was Dr. Casey Smith and the nurse was Jamie Miller, RN.

9. On arrival at the emergency department on March 11, YR-2, Nurse Jamie Miller, RN, noted that Timmy had an elevated heart and respiratory rate and that his temperature at that time revealed an ongoing fever. Nurse Miller communicated these findings to Dr. Smith.

10. Dr. Smith's March 11, YR-2, initial physical examination revealed increased work of breathing and an elevated temperature between 103 and 104 degrees Fahrenheit, with other abnormal vital signs noted.

11. Timmy's grandmother, Jules Avila, joined her daughter and grandson at the hospital during Dr. Smith's examination and stated more than once that Timmy was lethargic.

12. Dr. Smith ordered Tylenol and a nebulizer treatment for Timmy at that time.

13. Dr. Smith ordered a chest x-ray, which was performed at approximately 10:00 p.m. The results were unremarkable.

14. Timmy was monitored in the ED from approximately 9:00 p.m. until 4:15 a.m. on March 11–12, YR-2, with what was believed to be a viral upper respiratory infection and cough. This monitoring consisted of Jamie Miller, RN, intermittently checking Timmy's vital signs. After the initial dose of Tylenol and the nebulizer treatment, administered at approximately 9:15 p.m., and the chest x-ray performed at approximately 10:00 p.m., no other medication was given nor tests were performed during

this monitoring, despite plaintiff mother Shirley Jones informing Nurse Miller that she believed Timmy was becoming lethargic.

15. At approximately 4:15 a.m. on March 12, Timmy began to complain that his neck hurt. Shirley Jones summoned Nurse Miller, who examined Timmy and called for Dr. Smith.

16. At approximately 4:30 a.m. on March 12, Dr. Smith arrived. Upon examining Timmy, he ordered blood work and a lumbar puncture. Dr. Smith also ordered IV antibiotics, which were started before the test results were returned. The results of these tests showed bacterial meningitis.

17. When he arrived at the ED, Timmy was given an inadequate work up. No blood work or other diagnostic studies were performed. Instead, the medical staff simply presumed a diagnosis of a viral upper respiratory infection and bronchiolitis.

18. Due to a substantial delay in the diagnosis of meningitis, Timmy has sustained permanent deafness secondary to the defendant's negligence.

COUNT I

V. PLAINTIFF V. DEFENDANT

19. Plaintiffs incorporate paragraphs 1 through 16, inclusive, as though set forth at length herein.

20. The negligence and carelessness of defendant includes the following:

    a. failing to take a proper, thorough, and accurate history relating to the minor plaintiff, including the minor plaintiff's signs and symptoms prior to presentation to the ED;

    b. failing to take heed of plaintiff Shirley Avila's concerns relating to the medical condition of the minor plaintiff;

    c. failing to perform a proper workup of the minor plaintiff's medical condition at the time of presentation, which would have included appropriate blood work, cultures, lumbar puncture, radiological testing, and other forms of evaluation that should have been performed consistent with the standard of care;

    d. failing to properly diagnose and treat the minor plaintiff's compromised medical condition during the presentations to the ED on March 11, YR-2, into March 12, YR-2;

    e. misdiagnosing the minor plaintiff's medical condition as an upper respiratory infection instead of recognizing the seriousness of the minor plaintiff's medical condition, including the bacterial meningitis from which he was suffering;

f. failing to properly and timely order, diagnose, and interpret various forms of testing that were provided to the minor plaintiff during the treatment in question;

g. failing to consult with other specialists to facilitate prompt diagnosis and treatment of plaintiff's medical condition;

h. failing to timely order appropriate prophylactic antibiotics in light of the minor plaintiff's medical condition;

i. failing to take all reasonable and appropriate measures so as not to increase the risk of harm to the minor plaintiff by delay in the diagnosis and treatment of the minor plaintiff's condition upon his visit to the ED;

j. failing to properly recognize the foreseeable risks of injury to the minor plaintiff in light of his clinical history and his presentation, as well as the information provided by the minor plaintiff's mother throughout the treatment;

k. failing to comply with the accepted standards of care to ensure that the minor plaintiff's condition was timely diagnosed and properly treated to prevent and decrease the risk of injury;

l. failing to adhere to hospital practices, policies, and procedures as described herein to ensure that the minor plaintiff's condition would be timely and properly diagnosed;

m. failing to properly assess and/or examine the minor plaintiff during the treatment in question;

n. failing to coordinate the minor plaintiff's timely care and treatment with various providers at defendant Nita City Hospital to ensure timely diagnosis and treatment of his condition;

o. failing to adequately assess, document, and intervene to promptly diagnose and treat the minor plaintiff's condition;

p. failing to timely diagnose and treat the minor plaintiff's deteriorating medical condition, which the defendant knew or should have known about during the time he was a patient at Nita City Hospital; and

21. Defendant Nita City Hospital is vicariously liable for the negligence and carelessness of its agents and/or employees, including the individual defendants identified in this Complaint, with respect to the treatment in question.

22. As a direct and proximate result of the defendant's negligence and carelessness, minor plaintiff Timmy Avila has suffered the following severe, catastrophic, and permanent injuries.

a. As a direct and proximate result of the defendant's negligence and carelessness, minor plaintiff has in the past suffered, and will in the future continue to suffer, severe pain, suffering, mental anguish, emotional distress, disfigurement, embarrassment in human relations, and loss of enjoyment of life and life's pleasures, all to his great detriment and loss.

b. As a direct and proximate result of the defendant's negligence and carelessness, the minor plaintiff and his mother have in the past, and will in the future, require substantial medical treatment; and he has incurred and will continue to incur substantial medical expenses in an effort to treat his injuries, to plaintiffs' great detriment and loss.

c. As a direct and proximate result of the defendant's negligence and carelessness, the minor plaintiff will in the future incur a substantial wage loss, to minor plaintiff's great detriment and loss.

WHEREFORE, plaintiffs respectfully request judgment in their favor and against the defendant in the amount in excess of the applicable arbitration limits, including interests, costs of suit, delay damages, and such other relief as this Honorable Court may deem appropriate.

Date: January 9, YR-1

Jackie T. Thomas

Thomas Law Associates
Jackie T. Thomas, Esquire
1229 Chestnut Street
Nita City, Nita 57815
819-555-7423
Attorney for Plaintiffs

IN THE DARROW COUNTY
COURT OF COMMON PLEAS

SHIRLEY AVILA, AS PARENT AND NATURAL GUARDIAN ON BEHALF OF HER MINOR SON, TIMOTHY AVILA,	:	Case No. 17-108
	:	**THIS IS NOT AN ARBITRATION**
Plaintiffs	:	**JURY TRIAL DEMANDED**
v.	:	
NITA CITY HOSPITAL, Defendant	:	

ANSWER WITH AFFIRMATIVE DEFENSES OF DEFENDANT WITH NEW MATTER OF NITA CITY HOSPITAL TO PLAINTIFFS' COMPLAINT

Defendant, Nita City Hospital, by and through its attorneys, respectfully submits the following Answer with Affirmative Defenses to Plaintiffs' Complaint and respectfully requests judgment to be entered in its favor.

1–22. In the interest of brevity and to avoid repetition, all allegations except as to agency are denied as stated and as legal conclusions. Strict proof is demanded at trial.

AFFIRMATIVE DEFENSES

23. Answering defendant hereby incorporates, by reference, its response to paragraphs 1 through 20 of plaintiffs' complaint.
24. Plaintiffs' claims may be barred or limited by plaintiff's comparative negligence.
25. Plaintiffs' claims may be barred by plaintiff's contributory negligence.
26. Plaintiffs' claims may be barred by the fact that plaintiff assumed the risk of the injuries and/or damages alleged herein.
27. Plaintiffs' claims may be barred by the applicable statute of limitations.
28. Plaintiffs may have failed to state a cause of action upon which relief can be granted.
29. The acts of answering defendant alleged to constitute negligence were not substantial causes or factors in the injuries and/or damages claimed in this case.
30. The injuries and/or damages, all of which are expressly denied, may have been caused by plaintiffs' failure to mitigate the damages.

31. Answering defendant reserves the right to assert all other affirmative defenses under Nita Rule of Civil Procedure 1030 to the extent that further investigation or discovery reveals any such defenses may be pertinent.

WHEREFORE, answering defendant, Nita City Hospital, respectfully requests that judgment be entered in its favor and against plaintiffs, with costs and counsel fees.

Date: January 18, YR-1

Mickey N. Plane

Harrison, Plane & Bennett, LLP
Mickey N. Plane, Esquire
3320 Market Street
Nita City, Nita 57815
(819) 555-3729
Attorney for Defendant

DEPOSITIONS

Deposition of Shirley Avila

My name is Shirley Avila. I am twenty-five years old. I currently reside at 2215 Market Street in Nita City, Nita, with my son, Timmy. Timmy is four years old. I graduated from West Nita high school in YR-7, then went to Nita Community College for a couple years. I didn't get a degree from NCC—I took some business courses, but I had to work, too, and night school was just too much. Maybe I'll go back some day.

I met Timmy's father, Tony, at NCC, just before I stopped taking classes. He seemed like a nice guy, and we dated on and off for about a year, nothing serious. Then I got pregnant. Tony flipped out. He broke up with me because he thought I was trying to trap him into marriage. We didn't talk for almost seven months, but by the time Timmy was born, Tony wanted to be part of his life. He'd come by and see Timmy every couple weeks. That was before the hospital destroyed our lives. Timmy's father is no longer in the picture. Being a single mom is not easy; I work an office job during the day and as a waitress a few nights per week to make ends meet. My parents watch Timmy for me when I work in the evenings. No, Tony doesn't pay any child support. I'd have to go to court and get a court order, and I don't have the money to hire an attorney or the time to go to court.

It was scary to think about having a baby so young, but having Timmy was the greatest thing that ever happened to me. I didn't think that I was ready to be a mom; Timmy taught me just as much as I taught him. He was full of energy, even as an infant. He loved to play with the children at daycare. My folks would always joke that we had a star NFL quarterback in the making because of how much Timmy loved to throw the football. And when Timmy would finally tire himself out, at the very end of the night, I'd sit him on my lap, and we'd fall asleep together watching television.

Timmy never had a problem with his hearing up until I brought him to Nita City Hospital in March YR-2. When he was born in January YR-4, the hospital staff gave him a hearing test, and they told me that Timmy passed and that his hearing was perfectly normal. When Timmy was a baby and I would call him, or his grandparents would talk to him, Timmy would always respond.

On March 8, YR-2, Timmy woke up with a little bit of a cold and a fever. His nose was running, and he was congested. I checked his temperature, and it was just a little over 99 degrees. At that point, I didn't call a doctor or anything like that. It didn't seem serious, and kids catch colds, you know? Still, like any parent, I felt bad for the poor little guy. I couldn't take him to daycare, even though that's probably where he caught it, so I asked my folks if they could watch him for the day, because I had to work.

When I picked him up that evening, he was definitely cranky and uncomfortable. I gave him Tylenol. He settled down after that; he slept well that night. When he woke up still sick the next day, March 9, I got a little more concerned. He was still congested, with a runny nose. Timmy also had no appetite; I was having a tough time feeding him.

No matter what I gave him, he just pushed it away. I checked his temperature, and his fever was running up to 104 degrees. I called the hospital's care consultation number to talk to a nurse—they really encourage you to do that instead of coming right into the emergency room. I don't remember who I talked to, but they said to keep an eye on him, but that he was OK if his fever came down when I gave him Tylenol. I can't remember if I gave them my name or not.

It was a long day, let me tell you. Timmy was bored, but didn't have enough energy to play. We watched Disney movies, curled up on the couch. At bedtime, he was fussy, but let me rock him to sleep after another dose of Tylenol.

When he woke up the same on March 10, YR-2, that's when I got really nervous. My car is broken down, and I don't have the money to repair it, so I called my mom and asked her to drive Timmy and me to the Nita City Hospital Emergency Department. When they checked, his fever was 104 degrees. They asked me whether he was peeing and pooping like normal. I hadn't thought about it until then, but we hadn't been going through nearly as many diapers, and I told the nurse that. My mom said that they should put him in a tepid bath, but they ignored her and just gave him more Tylenol. She was unhappy with that and let them know, but Timmy's fever went back down. After about three hours, they told us to take him home because he just had a cold.

On March 11, YR-2, Timmy woke up still sick, but we'd been to the hospital and they'd said it was just a cold, so I kept giving him Tylenol. I had to go to work that day, so Mom came over and watched him. When I got home, she said she'd given Timmy a couple tepid baths during the day and his fever was down—he'd even played a little in the bathtub. I thanked her, and she went home. I tried to feed Timmy dinner, but he wouldn't eat anything. He kept turning away and pushing the food away. He drank a little juice, but barely any. After dinner, we sat down on the couch and I put on The Lion King for, like, the millionth time. Timmy curled up beside me. I was so tired; I think I dozed off for a while. When I woke back up, I noticed that Timmy's breathing sounded weird and really fast. I felt his forehead and realized he was burning up. He was kind of glassy-eyed, too. I went from concerned to scared. I tried to call my mom, but she wasn't answering, so I called 9-1-1 and told them to send an ambulance. Like I said, my car wasn't working—it needs a new transmission—and I couldn't get ahold of my mom.

The ambulance arrived around 8:30 p.m. on March 11, YR-2. The EMS workers were checking Timmy over when my Mom arrived—she'd been at the movies, and when she got out and saw a bunch of calls from me, she drove right over. Mom got completely hysterical. She was yelling at the EMS workers to look at Timmy, couldn't they see he was lethargic. The EMS workers tried to ignore her and get me to answer their questions. It was so chaotic, I never even considered letting my mom drive us to the hospital. The ambulance took Timmy and me to the emergency room at Nita City Hospital. The whole ride, Timmy was breathing fast and kind of gasping. The hospital was only fifteen minutes away, but that ride felt like an eternity. The EMS worker put a mask over Timmy's face. I didn't know if they were giving him oxygen or some other treatment. I answered the

EMS workers questions in the ambulances and told them again about Timmy's symptoms, that Timmy had a fever, wasn't eating as much, and was lethargic.

When we got to the emergency room around 9:00 p.m., they wheeled Timmy straight back into a room. At that point, Nurse Miller was waiting, and I told her everything that had happened since I'd been at the hospital the day before: that Timmy's cold and fever had gotten much worse and that now he was breathing really fast. She asked me about his eating and drinking, and I told him that he was cranky and wouldn't eat or drink anything. I told her that I'd only had to change his diaper a couple times that day because he was dry. Dr. Smith came in a few minutes later, and I told him how Timmy had gotten worse since we'd been at the ED the day before. The doctor ordered a chest x-ray and examined Timmy with a stethoscope. My mother arrived about then, while the doctor was examining Timmy, and said to the nurse and Dr. Smith that Timmy seemed lethargic. After they examined him, Dr. Smith told me that the x-ray came back as normal and that Timmy had an upper respiratory infection. Dr. Smith wanted to keep Timmy at the hospital to monitor him, but said that I should not worry because this was a very common problem. Dr. Smith had ordered Tylenol for Timmy's fever and a nebulizer for the breathing, and my little boy was breathing easier by this time. I told the doctor that I was staying the night with Timmy; I wasn't about to leave his side. At first, Timmy did seem to be getting a bit better with the medicine. He fell asleep for a while, and I pushed a chair up by the bed and laid my head on the mattress, trying to sleep.

I woke up a while later, startled. It's that Mom intuition, I think. I could immediately tell that Timmy was worse. His breathing was even faster. I tried to wake him up, but he wasn't responding to me at all. Timmy seemed lethargic, but it was the middle of the night, when he was usually asleep, so I debated whether I was overreacting. Dr. Smith came back to check on Timmy just before midnight. I told the doctor that Timmy seemed sluggish, but Dr. Smith told me not to worry, that it was under control. Dr. Smith ordered more Tylenol for Timmy. Dr. Smith seemed in a hurry. Within a few minutes after arriving to check on Timmy, Dr. Smith left the room and hustled down the hallway. Neither Dr. Smith nor anyone else at the hospital gave Timmy any more treatment or medicine at that point.

I decided to trust Dr. Smith, which turned out to be the worst decision of my life. Timmy stayed basically the same over the next few hours. I put my head back down on the mattress and dozed off and on—not much, because I was listening to Timmy. The change in his breathing was gradual, so I wasn't sure I was really hearing it, but now when Timmy would breathe, sometimes he would let out a little moan. I just kept telling myself the same thing—that Dr. Smith had it under control. Close to 4:00 a.m., I woke up again when Timmy moaned loudly. I leaned over him and said, "Timmy, what's wrong?" Timmy put his hand on his neck and began to whimper. I said: "Is it your neck? Is that what hurts?" Timmy nodded his head. He opened his eyes to look at me, and his eyes started to cross. I decided enough was enough; I ran out into the hall and found Nurse Miller. Nurse Miller took one look at Timmy and immediately got Dr. Smith to come to Timmy's room. I told Dr. Smith about Timmy's neck pain, Timmy's moaning, and that it looked like his eyes were crossing.

Dr. Smith ordered blood work and performed a lumbar puncture. Dr. Smith said the tests would tell us whether this was just an upper respiratory issue or if it was something a little more serious, like a bacterial infection. It was almost 5:00 a.m. by then. I helped the nurses hold Timmy still while Dr. Smith performed the lumbar puncture on my baby boy. I could barely watch as they put that needle into Timmy's lower back, and I was so proud of him for being brave.

They also drew blood for a blood test. When the results came back, Dr. Smith told me that the blood test showed that Timmy had an abnormal level of white blood cells and had a high C-reactive protein level. I did not know what that meant. When I asked him to explain, Dr. Smith said that the lumbar puncture showed that Timmy had bacterial meningitis and not an upper respiratory infection like Dr. Smith had originally thought.

After they diagnosed Timmy with bacterial meningitis, Dr. Smith wanted to keep Timmy at the hospital for a few weeks for precautionary reasons. I can't tell you how hellish it is to have to leave your baby alone in a hospital room, but I had to go back to work—no one else was going to pay my rent. For a while, Timmy slept a lot. I was taking extra shifts at the restaurant because I needed the money to make up for the time I'd missed at work. Most evenings, by the time the bus dropped me off at the hospital, Timmy was already asleep. My parents came to visit him as much as they could, but then Mom got a bad cold and they couldn't risk infecting him, so they weren't around as much as I'd like. Tony said he went to see Timmy a couple times, but we never crossed paths—he's never seen Timmy since. So Timmy was just with the hospital staff for a lot of March. I guess that's why we didn't notice anything for so long.

At the end of March, Mom called me to say that she thought something was wrong with Timmy. She'd called a few other times, early on, that were false alarms, so I didn't rush down to the hospital that day. I got there on Saturday, when I finally had a day off. Timmy was happy to see me, but then he ignored me, playing with some blocks on his table. I thought he was mad at me for not being around. I felt so guilty. I stacked the blocks, and he knocked them down and laughed. His laugh sounded kind of different, but I figured that was part of the recovery. We played that game for a while, and then Timmy went back to ignoring me. I asked the nurse how he was doing, and she said that he was a very quiet boy, but sweet and smiley. By the time I left that evening, I had a feeling in the pit of my stomach that something was wrong. I just wanted to ignore it and pretend it wasn't there. But I was right.

Sometime in early April, Dr. Smith ordered a hearing test for Timmy. When I arrived that evening, I asked about the results. I know nurses aren't supposed to give out that kind of information, but I could tell by the look I got that the news was bad. I asked directly, and one of the nurses told me Timmy failed. The tests said that Timmy had suffered nerve damage as a result of the bacterial meningitis, and as a result of that nerve damage, Timmy is now deaf. I slid down the wall, crying. Just as I thought we were getting close to getting our lives back to normal, I learned that they will never be normal again.

Timmy's life will never be the same. Even with the frequent visits to the ENT and the audiologist, he isn't getting better. Timmy has to go to a special school for deaf children, and unless he improves, he may have to stay at that special school through high school. Timmy has to wear hearing aids, but they don't seem to help either. The doctors tell me to consider a cochlear implant for Timmy, but I don't want to see Timmy be put through any more than he's been through. The doctors said that surgery can have serious side effects—including a risk of meningitis. Sometimes the implants get infected, or they aren't placed right, and it means more surgery. Hasn't Timmy already been through enough the first time? In my opinion, the doctors and nurses at Nita City Hospital just didn't take Timmy's condition seriously until it was too late, and they're acting like it can all be made OK by sticking a machine inside his head. They are so callous. It makes me furious. I want to destroy Nita City Hospital and everyone who works there for what they did to Timmy.

The school keeps asking me to take their sign language course, but when am I supposed to do that? I have to work even longer hours now, because it costs to have Timmy in that school. Even with tuition paid for, there are just lots of expenses for transportation and equipment and enrichment extras they tell me he needs. I want the best for my son, but I'm just one person. The sign language makes me so sad. It's always going to leave him at a disadvantage. I want him to learn to read lips so that he can get along in the world. That's what we work on at home.

Yes, it's true that Tony's visits with Timmy were getting fewer and further between even before the hospital—but now there's no chance of rebuilding that relationship. I don't even know where Tony's living anymore.

No, I didn't have a regular pediatrician for Timmy before this all happened. I told you how much I have to work; I'm never available for normal doctor's office hours. Timmy has insurance through the state, so the hospital gets paid. There's no reason they can't give him his vaccinations and such when we come in there.

Yes, I did get a ticket for neglect when Timmy was only a couple months old. It was the stupidest thing ever. I needed to get some cash from the ATM, but it was the late in the afternoon on Labor Day, so the drive-through ATM was out of money. It was pouring down rain, and I didn't want to take Timmy out in it. I pulled my car right up in front of the bank and ran into the vestibule, where they had a walk-up ATM. I could see the car the whole time, and I had locked it. But this cop came along and gave me a ticket for leaving a baby unaccompanied in a car. I couldn't believe it! The judge told me that if I pled no contest to the misdemeanor, he would just assign me to a parenting class, but if I tried to fight the charge, social services might take away my baby. I was so scared! Of course I pled no contest and took that class. I passed with flying colors—I'm not a neglectful mother at all.

Shirley Avila
Shirley Avila

April 30, YR-1

Deposition of Jules Avila

My name is Jules Avila. I am seventy-one years old. I currently reside with my spouse, Frankie, at 1907 Market Street in a one bedroom apartment. I've lived in Nita City all of my life.

I used to work at the Nita City Navigators baseball games as an usher, but I retired a few years back after my grandson, Timmy, lost his hearing. Ever since then, I do my best to spend as much time with Timmy as possible. Timmy's mother, Shirley, is my daughter, and it has been hard for her ever since Timmy was diagnosed with hearing loss back in YR-2. You see, Shirley and Timmy's father had a bit of a rocky relationship. They split up when Shirley was pregnant with Timmy, and Timmy's father would only see Timmy occasionally, maybe once every few weeks. But ever since Timmy lost his hearing, Timmy's father stopped coming around. So, on evenings when Shirley works, or when she just needs a break, I will have Timmy at my apartment, or I'll go to Shirley's house.

I used to spend a lot of time with Timmy, even before he lost his hearing. Everyone says how great it is to have grandchildren, but Timmy really was a joy. He was a really energetic boy. When the Navigators were away, or during the offseason, I would have lunch with Timmy and Shirley at least a couple of times per week. Timmy loved my famous grilled cheese, and he'd wash the sandwich down with a big glass of chocolate milk. He really was a smart boy, too. I would always joke that Timmy was going to be a star quarterback just like Bart Starr or Johnny Unitas, and if that didn't work out, he could always become an astronaut or a scientist. He really had so many talents.

That being said, like any grandparent, I worried about Timmy. March 11, YR-2, wasn't the first time Timmy had been to Nita City Hospital. From the time Timmy was one year old right up until he was admitted to Nita City Hospital on March 11, YR-2, I myself had taken Timmy to Nita City Hospital on at least seven or eight occasions. When Timmy would have a fever that lingered a little too long, or I thought his heart was beating fast after he would run around my living room, or if I just thought Timmy wasn't acting like himself, I would put him in my car and take him to Nita City Hospital. It actually was a little bit of a source of tension between Shirley and me. The last time that I took Timmy to the emergency room, in January YR-2 (I think he had a cough that had lasted a couple of days), Shirley said: "He's fine! This is getting ridiculous—he's been to the hospital three times in a month for nothing! I can't believe the people at the hospital even listen to us when we take him there anymore." Several times when I took Timmy to Nita City Hospital, he was seen by Nurse Miller and Dr. Smith. I actually got to know them pretty well over that year. Each time I took Timmy to Nita City Hospital, they ran some tests, asked some questions, and sent Timmy home. They always said there was nothing wrong with him and that he was perfectly healthy.

That's why when Shirley and I were actually in agreement about taking Timmy to the hospital, it was different. Shirley dropped Timmy off at my house on the morning of March 8,

YR-2. She said that Timmy was a little bit sick and he just didn't seem like himself. He had a slight fever and a snotty nose. She said to call her at work if I needed to.

Timmy stayed at my apartment until 8:00 that night. Shirley had to work late, but I didn't mind—I wanted to take care of Timmy, especially since he was sick. Early in the day, Timmy actually seemed normal. Shirley told me that had given him Tylenol before she dropped him off, and so that wasn't surprising. However, I noticed that later that day Timmy was less energetic, and his head felt warm. I took his temperature, and sure enough, his temperature was 101.1F. I got especially worried when Timmy wouldn't eat my grilled cheese, which he absolutely loves. I put the grilled cheese in front of him, and he pushed it away. I was absolutely shocked. I sent Frankie out to the pharmacy for some baby Tylenol. After I gave that to Timmy, his fever went down and he nibbled a little at his grilled cheese and drank some juice, but I could tell he still wasn't feeling well. I considered taking him to the emergency room, but Frankie talked me out of it, saying that Shirley would be furious and that I was overreacting.

When Shirley finally got to my house around 8:00 p.m. on March 8, YR-2, I told her what I had observed. I told her that Timmy wouldn't eat. Shirley said, "I couldn't get him to eat breakfast, either." The two of us agreed that if Timmy didn't seem better the next day, we needed to call the hospital.

I called Shirley early the next morning, on March 9, YR-2. She said that Timmy's fever was even higher. She had called the hospital's care consultation number to talk to a nurse and that they told her to give Timmy some Tylenol and see if it helped before taking Timmy to the ED. I told her I would check in later on to see how Timmy was. She called me back after she put Timmy to bed, around 7:30 p.m. She told me that Timmy had sat on the couch with her all day and watched television and he was a little fussy before bedtime, but eventually fell asleep after some more Tylenol. I felt somewhat relieved, but like any grandparent, not fully. I said, "Shirley, if he's not back to normal by tomorrow, we need to go to Nita City Hospital." Shirley reluctantly agreed.

On March 10, YR-2, Shirley called around 9:00 a.m. She said Timmy still had a fever, wasn't eating his breakfast, and she was still concerned. She asked if I could drive her and Timmy to Nita City Hospital. I think I was already in the car on the way to their home before she could even hang up the phone. When we got to Nita City Hospital, the nurses checked Timmy out, and his fever was 104 degrees. I said that they should put him in a tepid bath—that's what I always did when Shirley was sick—but they ignored me and just gave him more Tylenol. Timmy's fever went back down. After about three hours, they told us to take him home because he just had a cold.

The next day, March 11, YR-2, Shirley asked me to come over to watch Timmy, since she had to go to work again. Even though he still had a fever, Timmy actually seemed a little bit better. He took a few bites of his grilled cheese, and he seemed a little livelier than he had been the past few days. I gave him a bath—that was our favorite activity. I was relieved when Timmy started to smile and giggle and play with his bath toys. Finally, it seemed like Timmy was back to his normal self. I left Shirley's house around 6:00 p.m., after she got home from work. I was going to see a movie with Frankie, and I know how much Frankie hates to miss the previews. When we got to the theatre, I realized I'd left my phone at home. Frankie doesn't have a cell phone—always says the words on the phone's screen are too small. I told Frankie to just make the words bigger, like on my phone, but Frankie would just say, "Who has the time?" For someone who has been retired for fifteen years, Frankie sure is a busy person.

We got home after the movie, around 8:30 p.m. I checked my cell phone and saw five or six missed calls. They were all from Shirley. My heart sank. When I called her back twice and she didn't answer, I rushed over to Shirley's house. I saw the ambulance out front, and I saw my grandson inside the ambulance and the EMS workers were checking on him. By this point, there were a crowd of neighbors outside of the ambulance. I pushed through everyone and went right up to the ambulance where Timmy was. He was just lying there on the stretcher, his little arms and legs flopped limply and his head rolled to one side. I started to scream: "This isn't Timmy! This isn't my grandson! Can't you see how lifeless and weak he is?" Shirley told me that they wouldn't let me ride in the ambulance with them, but I could meet her and Timmy at Nita City Hospital.

I got to the hospital around 9:15 p.m., and Shirley and Timmy were already there. It took me a little while to talk the front desk nurse into letting me go back to the room, but I wasn't about to be turned away—that's my grandson, and grandparents have rights. I think Nurse Miller must have remembered me, because I am pretty sure I saw Nurse Miller look at Dr. Smith and roll her eyes, but I am really not sure. Nurse Miller came right over to me and said hello, then asked me if I was enjoying my last few weeks of vacation before baseball season started again. I forgot that I had talked to Nurse Miller on a few occasions over the past month or so about my job while she was evaluating Timmy.

I had met Dr. Smith a few times before, too. Aside from the times I had been to Nita City Hospital, Dr. Smith's son plays little league baseball for a local team. Dr. Smith's son's team got to play in the stadium that the Navigators play in for the Nita City Little League Championship. This was in June YR-3. Dr. Smith sat in my section for the championship game. I actually seated Dr. Smith myself. In the ninth inning of a tie game, his son's team had the bases loaded. His son was rounding third base, and the third base coach yelled for him to stop at third. I don't know what happened, but his son kept running, ignoring the third base coach, and was called out at home plate. It cost the team the game. Everyone was really getting on Dr. Smith's son. Dr. Smith finally got up out of the seat, face reddened, neck veins popping out, and yelled: "He didn't hear him! Obviously he couldn't hear him!" It got really heated between Dr. Smith and another parent, so much so that Dr. Smith smacked the guy. Security had to escort Dr. Smith out of the stadium. Dr. Smith used some language that I am not comfortable repeating on the way out. I heard through the grapevine that Dr. Smith got an assault conviction for that incident. I guess people really care about baseball in Nita City.

Anyway, Dr. Smith was examining Timmy by the time I got there, and I think Nurse Miller was talking to me about baseball to keep me out of the way. But I'm too smart for that. I ignored her and paid attention to the doctor, so the nurse went back to writing in Timmy's chart.

Shirley told Dr. Smith that Timmy had a fever for days, hadn't been eating, and was breathing funny. Shirley told Dr. Smith that these symptoms had been lingering for a few days. Again, I said, "Wait, wait, wait, what about him being sluggish, he's really sluggish and weak, he's not himself." Shirley said, "He is definitely a little sluggish, doctor." Nurse Miller was writing something in the chart and didn't say anything to me. I guess she was writing down what I said, but I am not sure. Dr. Smith didn't say anything. Then again, Dr. Smith was listening to Timmy's chest with a stethoscope at this point. I don't remember if I ever mentioned the fact that Timmy was sluggish again to anyone at Nita City Hospital, but this was the one time that I remember it vividly.

Dr. Smith ordered a chest x-ray. Before they took him for the x-ray, Nurse Miller gave Timmy Tylenol and a nebulizer. I'll admit, Timmy did seem a little better at first. When Dr. Smith came back to report the results of the chest x-ray, I told Dr. Smith how worried I was, that Timmy didn't seem like himself and that I thought this was more serious than just a chest issue. Dr. Smith responded: "I know how worried you are about Timmy, but trust me, just like last time, Timmy is perfectly fine. Just a respiratory infection. We're going to monitor him overnight, just to be safe. He'll be back home in the morning. Don't be worried!" I trusted Dr. Smith. Shirley told me that she had it under control and that I should go home. I had employee orientation the next morning at the baseball stadium, and I needed to be up early. I left the hospital around 11:00 p.m. I didn't see Nurse Miller after 9:30 p.m.

The next day, Shirley called me on my lunch break to tell me that the doctor had diagnosed Timmy with bacterial meningitis. I didn't really know what that meant. Shirley said that Dr. Smith wanted to keep Timmy at the hospital for a few weeks for precautionary reasons. I was there as much as I could be, but me and Frankie got a bad cold a week or so after Timmy was diagnosed, and we agreed that it would be better for us to stay away from Timmy until I was better. One day in late March, I was staying with Timmy at the hospital while Shirley was working, and I noticed something strange. Timmy wasn't really answering me when I called him the first time. I had to sort of speak up, clap my hands, or something like that to get his attention. I called Shirley to tell her that something was wrong with Timmy. I think Shirley thought I was just being my worrisome self. I wish that was true.

When I heard that Timmy had lost his hearing, I couldn't believe it. My poor grandson will never be able to live a normal life. He's not the same Timmy that I knew. I know that the doctors wanted Timmy to get a cochlear implant to improve his hearing, and there's a chance his hearing might come back, but there are no guarantees. I don't want my grandson to be put through any more than he's been through already. I should have never left that hospital. I should have never left Timmy alone with Dr. Smith.

Jules Avila

Jules Avila

May 9, YR-1

Deposition of Jamie Miller, RN

My name is Jamie Miller. I am thirty-eight years old. I have been a registered nurse since YR-15. I worked at Nita City Hospital from YR-7 until YR-1. I have my Bachelor's degree in Nursing from Saint Joseph's University. I have several certifications, such as Basic Life Support (BLS), Advanced Cardiovascular Life Support (ACLS), and Pediatric Advanced Life Support (PALS). Currently, I am pursuing a masters in Nursing from University of Nita and am also in the process of earning a certificate from the American Association of Nurse Anesthetists to be a Certified Registered Nurse Anesthetist (CRNA). I left Nita City Hospital last year to become a full-time student. I also had been accused of stealing painkillers from the hospital. I didn't do it, but the hospital told me that if I left, they wouldn't press charges.

I worked in the emergency department at Nita City Hospital. An emergency nurse is exactly what it sounds like. I work primarily in the emergency department of a hospital. We treat patients in emergency situations. Emergency nurses are trained to recognize urgent or life-threatening conditions in patients. I consider myself a specialist in emergency medicine. I am certified in emergency pediatric medicine. My typical shift at Nita City Hospital was 7:00 p.m. to 7:00 a.m. I usually worked three days per week.

I am very familiar with Timmy Avila. His grandmother brought him to the emergency room every time he had the slightest sniffle or rash, and his mother brought him more than a few times. We always provide the finest care, but it gets frustrating when people like this continually show up in the ED. That's not what emergency care is for, and when they're taking up a bed in our space for something that they should go to a regular doctor for, it means that someone who is in real distress has to wait that much longer for care. Plus, it's a little bit like the boy who cried wolf, you know?

Of course I took it completely seriously when they brought Timmy in by ambulance. The medic reported that Timmy had a fever of 104 degrees Fahrenheit. The medic also told me that Timmy seemed irritable. When the medic gave me her report, she said that the EMS team gave Timmy a nebulizer treatment in the ambulance for Timmy's wheezing. Shirley Avila told me Timmy had a fever and had been coughing for a few days. She told me that she had brought Timmy to the ED on the previous day, March 10, so I pulled up those records. I confirmed with Ms. Avila that Timmy continued to have the decreased urination and decreased oral intake she had reported the day before. Nothing that I observed led me to doubt the accuracy of those symptoms, though I myself did not observe Timmy being irritable, as the medic had told me. I don't recall Timmy's mother, or anyone for that matter, telling me that Timmy was lethargic.

My examination of Timmy confirmed what the EMS medic and Timmy's mother told me. Timmy did have a fever, was experiencing increased heart rate, increased work of breathing, and was wheezing. Everything else appeared to be normal. Based on what I learned through the EMS personnel and my own observations, I believed Timmy had an upper respiratory infection.

Dr. Smith came in to examine Timmy just as Timmy grandmother arrived. I'm not sure how she got back into the exam room—no one from the front desk will admit to letting her in. Maybe she followed another family in and no one realized. Timmy's grandmother is . . . well, let's just say that she can get a little hysterical when it comes to Timmy's health. I tried to run interference with her so that Dr. Smith could work, but she ignored me. Dr. Smith was trying to read the chart and ask Shirley Avila questions, and the grandmother kept interrupting everyone and fussing over Timmy. We all tried to ignore her and carry on. Dr. Smith finally got to examine Timmy. He listened to his chest with the stethoscope and checked Timmy's ears, throat, and nose. Based on his examination, he ordered a chest x-ray. This would have been around 10:00 p.m. After a dose of Tylenol and a nebulizer treatment, Timmy was taken to radiology and x-rayed, and we got the results back around 11:00 p.m. or so. It's true that the chest x-ray came back with no abnormalities. Still, we thought the issue was an upper respiratory infection. We decided to monitor Timmy overnight for the respiratory issues. Timmy appeared to be doing better in response to the Tylenol and nebulizer treatment.

From that point forward, around midnight or so, we decided we would continue to monitor Timmy overnight. To the best of my knowledge, there were no further tests ordered from that time. I know Shirley Avila says that she told hospital staff that Timmy seemed to be becoming more lethargic; I don't remember Ms. Avila saying anything like that to me, and I didn't make note of such an observation in my progress notes. Yes, I am aware that lethargy can be a symptom of meningitis, so I would have written it down.

Shirley Avila convinced her mother, Timmy's grandmother, to go home. Ms. Avila said that she would stay with Timmy for the night. That's pretty common up in pediatrics, and they have chairs that fold out to make a bed for the parent up there. We aren't set up for that in the ED, so Ms. Avila made do with the chair that was in the room. I closed the door so that the noise in the hall wouldn't keep her awake—even if I get frustrated with her misuse of the ED facilities, I'm still professional and sympathetic. I thought that rest was the best thing for both of them, so I only peeked in a couple times. I didn't take Timmy's vitals after midnight.

At 4:15 a.m., I saw Shirley Avila running down the hallway of the hospital towards me. Ms. Avila told me that Timmy was in a lot of pain. We ran back to Timmy's room. He was moaning, with his hand on his neck. I asked him if his neck hurt. Timmy nodded. I called Dr. Smith to evaluate Timmy. Dr. Smith arrived a few minutes after I called for him. Dr. Smith listened to Timmy's chest, then used the otoscope to look in the boy's ears and throat. When he asked Timmy to open his eyes, Timmy's eyes began to cross.

Dr. Smith immediately ordered blood work and performed a lumbar puncture. Both Dr. Smith and I agreed that further testing was necessary at this point. The blood work revealed a grossly abnormal white blood cell count and an elevated C–reactive protein level. The lumbar puncture revealed that Timmy had bacterial meningitis. Dr. Smith ordered IV antibiotics for Timmy, which we began administering immediately even before the lumbar puncture. Bacterial meningitis, as far as I know, can be treated successfully with antibiotics.

I am deeply saddened by what happened to Timmy Avila. Of course, you never want something like that to happen to a patient, especially one who is so young, like Timmy. But Dr. Smith and I did everything that we could have to treat Timmy. Even if we had diagnosed Timmy earlier, I still don't think the outcome would have changed, unfortunately. Timmy still would have suffered hearing loss, in my opinion.

I am familiar with the Nita City Hospital Children's Health Meningitis fact sheet, and I agree with everything contained within that sheet. However, the information contained in that document serves merely as guidelines. As an emergency nurse, you have to use your own judgment based on your experience. And based on my experience, there was nothing to suggest that Timmy had bacterial meningitis until the lumbar puncture and blood work were ordered after 4:00 a.m. on March 12, YR-2.

To prepare for this deposition, I reviewed my progress notes from March 11, YR-2, the EMS records, the results of Timmy's chest x-ray, the lab reports with respect to the tests administered to Timmy in the early hours of March 12, YR-2, the discharge summary, and the depositions of Dr. Smith, Shirley Avila, and Jules Avila.

Jamie Miller

Jamie Miller

July 7, YR-1

Jamie Miller, RN

Phone: (819)-555-966 jamie.miller@gnet.nita

Professional Nursing Experience

Nita City Hospital, Nita City, Nita (YR-7–YR-1)

Certified Nurse, Emergency Department

- Provide direct care to children and families in an emergency setting.
- Triage patients in order to determine patient acuity.
- Primary preceptor/instructor for graduate nurses.

Springfield Township Board of Education, Springfield, Nita (YR-9–YR-7)

Certified School Nurse, Springfield Middle School

- Independently assess and triage students with acute injuries and medical emergencies.
- Provide first aid and annual health screenings to approximately 600 middle school students.
- Work closely with school counselors and administrators in addressing and reporting cases of child abuse and neglect.
- Conduct training for staff related to needs of students with chronic medical conditions.
- Teach first aid classes to students.
- Collaborate with other nurses to develop district policies and procedures.

Nita City Pediatrics, Nita City, Nita (YR-12–YR-9)

Staff Nurse

- Provide health assessments, treatments, and immunization administration to infants, children, and adolescents in an ambulatory care setting.
- Provide parents with teaching such as newborn care, medication administration, and immunization administration.

Nita City Hospital, Nita City, Nita (YR-15–YR-12)

Staff Nurse, Oncology Unit

- Provide care for inpatient oncology and bone marrow transplant patients.
- Assist physicians with medical and surgical procedures.

Education

University of Nita, Nita City, Nita (YR-9)
Certificate in School Nursing

Saint Joseph's University, Philadelphia, PA (YR-15)
Bachelor's of Science in Nursing

Deposition of Dr. Casey Smith, MD

My name is Casey Smith. Currently, I am an attending physician at Nita City Hospital. I have been married to my spouse, Sandy, for twenty years, and we have three kids, ages eight, ten, and fourteen. Sandy and I met in high school, and we've been together since then. We've both lived in Nita City all our lives, except while I was in school. I received a bachelor's degree in biology with a minor in chemistry from Tufts University and went on to attend and graduate from Harvard Medical School. I am board certified in both pediatrics and pediatric emergency medicine.

Board certification requires a physician to demonstrate exceptional expertise in a particular specialty of medical practice. To become certified, I spent almost five years after medical school in supervised, in-practice training. I passed the rigorous testing and peer evaluation for both specialties, which was designed and administered by specialists in pediatrics and pediatric emergency medicine.

I was already familiar with Timmy Avila, thanks to his frequent visits. His grandmother in particular seemed to have a really high worry level about his health. We were all thorough, every time they brought Timmy in, of course. But we encouraged the Avilas to take more appropriate measures in seeking medical care.

On March 11, YR-2, Shirley and Timmy Avila arrived to the emergency room around 9:00 p.m. Timmy's mother told the floor nurse, Jamie Miller, that Timmy had a three-day history of 104F fever, a cough, runny nose, reduced oral intake, and reduced urinary output. On March 11, he developed further symptoms: increased work of breathing, rapid breathing, wheezing, irritability, and inconsolability. He had also been in the emergency department the day before. Nurse Miller relayed that information to me when I came into the room to examine Timmy. I ordered Tylenol and a nebulizer treatment for Timmy at that time.

Even though it helped, Timmy was still struggling. Around 10:00 p.m., I ordered a chest x-ray. The results of this test typically take about an hour or so to come back. The chest x-ray came back normal.

After evaluating Timmy and reviewing the results of the chest x-ray, I decided to pursue a viral respiratory based etiology. All of Timmy's symptoms were consistent with an upper respiratory infection, and though you can never be certain, this is a common problem with this type of presentation.

Yes, I do remember Timmy's grandmother coming into the examination room and kicking up a fuss while I was trying to examine Timmy and talk to his mother. I had to work hard to tune her out so I could focus on my evaluation. My experience with the grandmother is that her contributions are rarely helpful. I left Nurse Miller to listen to her and focused on Timmy and his mother. Nurse Miller filled out the initial intake form. I added my notes in the hospital database.

We did not order tests—such as a blood test, a lumbar puncture, or a urinalysis—to determine whether this was a bacterial infection. Those tests might have told us things that were indicative of a bacterial infection, such as an elevated white blood cell count or an elevated level of C-reactive protein. But there was no need to order those tests at the time; everything pointed to a respiratory infection. Yes, I do admit that rapid breathing and an abnormally high heart rate could be symptoms consistent with bacterial meningitis. Additionally, a respiratory infection, if not treated properly, can lead to bacterial meningitis. But those signs and symptoms are also entirely consistent with an upper respiratory infection. And yes, lethargy is considered a sign of bacterial meningitis, but I did not observe that Timmy was lethargic.

Children present in the ED regularly with symptoms identical to Timmy's. It would be a serious misuse of resources to perform lumbar punctures on every child. The procedure has its own risks, such as spinal fluid leakage and a small risk of infection or brain stem herniation. We do not perform this test lightly, and when I evaluated Timmy, my experience indicated to me that his condition did not warrant the procedure.

My plan was to monitor Timmy in the ED for a viral respiratory illness. As I said, I ordered Tylenol for Timmy's fever and a nebulizer treatment for his reported wheezing. Nurse Miller administered both the Tylenol and the nebulizer. I didn't consult with any other doctors, such as a physician in the infectious disease department, even though I could have. I was confident with the plan that we had in place. Timmy initially appeared to be doing better as a result of the administered Tylenol and nebulizer treatment.

Throughout the night, we continued to monitor Timmy. We didn't conduct any further tests or administer any more treatment. I know now that Shirley Avila claims she told me a number of times throughout the night that Timmy was lethargic, but I do not recall Ms. Avila ever once saying anything like that. Lethargy is a symptom of bacterial infection, and I certainly would have recorded that in my progress notes, which I didn't. I also know that the EMS records from the ambulance that Timmy and his mother took on March 11, YR-2, indicates that Timmy was lethargic, but I did not see those records until I became involved in this lawsuit.

Around 4:00 a.m., Nurse Miller paged me and said that Timmy was complaining of some neck pain. When I got to Timmy's room and began to evaluate him, Timmy's eyes were beginning to cross. Seeing this, I immediately ordered blood work and performed a lumbar puncture. Those tests were administered a little after 4:00 a.m. The blood work revealed a grossly abnormal white blood cell count and an elevated C-reactive protein level. The lumbar puncture showed that Timmy had bacterial meningitis. Once we suspected that Timmy had bacterial meningitis, we immediately administered antibiotics intravenously. The IV was started prior to the lumbar puncture. Bacterial meningitis, while serious, can be treated successfully with antibiotics.

As a result of the bacterial meningitis, I understand that Timmy has suffered permanent sensorineural hearing loss. I feel terrible for what happened to Timmy and what Timmy and his mother have had to endure. No family should go through such a traumatic experience. But even if we had administered antibiotics earlier, the outcome would have been substantially the same. Myself, the nurses, and everyone at Nita City Hospital did everything we should have done to treat Timmy.

I am familiar with the Nita City Hospital Children's Health Meningitis fact sheet, and I agree with everything contained within that sheet. But that sheet is a guideline, not a treatment regimen for every child who comes into the ED with a cold. The fact sheet cannot be substituted for hands-on clinical assessment and judgment, which is critical in the real world of emergency medicine.

Oh, Jules Avila told you about the incident at the ball park? I'm not surprised—she is a meddling woman. No, I didn't "smack" anybody. That other parent was in my face, screaming so hard that spit was hitting me in the cheek. It was offensive, and I pushed the jerk away from me, who stumbled back into the seats. It probably would have all been over then, except Jules Avila got hysterical and summoned the security guard. She insisted that the guard eject me—ridiculous, since the game was already over. But she likes drama. I did not receive an assault conviction. The other parent filed a civil assault case against me, and my insurance company settled it for a thousand dollars—I wanted to fight it, but they said settling was a much cheaper way to get rid of a nuisance suit like that.

To prepare for this deposition, I reviewed the progress notes from March 11, YR-2, the EMS records, the results of Timmy's chest x-ray, the lab reports with respect to the tests administered to Timmy in the early hours of March 12, YR-2, the discharge summary, and the deposition of Nurse Miller.

Casey Smith

Casey Smith

July 10, YR-1

Curriculum Vitae of Dr. Casey Smith, MD

EDUCATION

YR-21	BS	Tufts University (Biology; Chemistry (minor))
YR-17	MD	Harvard Medical School
YR-11	MSCE	University of Pennsylvania School of Medicine (Master of Science in Clinical Epidemiology)

POSTGRADUATE TRAINING and FACULTY APPOINTMENTS

YR-17–YR-16	Internship, Pediatrics—Nita City Hospital
YR-16–YR-14	Residency, Pediatrics—Nita City Hospital
YR-14–PRESENT	Assistant Professor, Pediatrics, Nita University
YR-14–PRESENT	Attending Physician, Children's American Medical Association

SPECIALITY CERTIFICATIONS and LICENSURE

YR-12	Pediatric Advanced Life Support
YR-11	National Advanced Life Support
YR-10	Advanced Trauma Life Support
YR-10	Board Certified, American Board of Pediatrics
YR-6	Board Certified, Pediatric Emergency Medicine Subspecialty
	Unrestricted Medical License, State of Nita

AWARDS, HONORS, and MEMBERSHIP IN HONORARY SOCIETIES

YR-23	National Science Foundation Grant
YR-22	Service Learning Project Grant, Drexel University
YR-10	Nicholas T. Potter Teaching Award (Nita City Hospital)
YR-9	Research Award, Best Poster, Nita City Hospital Research Institute

EDITORIAL AND PEER REVIEW POSITIONS

YR-14–PRESENT	Peer Reviewer—Society of Academic Emergency Medicine
YR-13–PRESENT	Peer Reviewer—Pediatric Emergency Care
YR-10–PRESENT	Peer Reviewer—Pediatric Academic Societies

BIBLIOGRAPHY AND RESEARCH PUBLICATIONS

- *Are emergency departments appropriately treating respiratory illness*? Annals of Pediatric Emergency Medicine 101:15, Jun., YR-12
- *Emergency department visits for viral infections in the United States*, Clinical Pediatric Emergency Medicine, Vol 27, No. 5, YR-11
- *Urgent care and testing in pediatric medicine*, Pediatric Emergency Care & Medicine Journal, Jan.–Mar., YR-9

Exhibits

Exhibit 1

Nita City Fire EMS

PATIENT: TIMMY AVILA

CALL

Call #: 64020372
Call Type: Difficulty Breathing
Crew: Lampone, Ray (Author); Gregory, Nicky (Driver)
Patient Name: Avila, Timmy
Sex: M
DOB: January 8, YR-4
Address: 2215 Market Street, Nita City, Nita

Date and Times March 11, YR-2 — **Notified**: 20:11; **Departed Qtrs**: 20:13; **At Scene**: 20:22; **At Patient**: 20:23; **Departed Scene**: 20:44; **At Destination**: 20:57; **Trip Distance**: 3 mi

SYMPTOMS

Hx PRESENT: Complaining of and symptoms consistent with Respir. breathing difficulty.
Hx PAST: Denies allergies, use of medication, and any preexisting condition.

NARRATIVE and FINDINGS

Arrived to find a 2-year-old patient in arms of his mother. Mother stated that patient has been sick with a cold and has had a fever as high as 104 for three days. Mother said she had been giving patient children's Tylenol. Mother said she called for an ambulance because patient was breathing fast, wasn't eating as much and was lethargic.

Patient was oriented and alert. Gag reflex was present. Observed labored breathing and wheezing. Apparent tachycardia. Temperature of skin was feverish. Temperature at 103.7. Color of skin was normal. Patient was crying and tearful.

Transported to Nita City Hospital where patient's care was transferred to an RN with report and without incident.

CARE EVENTS

Vitals - BP = 100/P, P = 170, R = 50, SaO2 = 100%
Motor skills intact, oriented verbally, obeys commands.
Transported to Nita City Hospital.

AUTHORIZATION

Ray Lampone
PARAMEDIC

Jamie Miller
NURSE

653 W. Starke Street, Nita City, Nita 47811

Phone: 819-555-4321 ✦ Fax: 819-555-4685

Exhibit 2

Nita City Hospital Intake Form	Doctor/Resident: Casey Smith Reporting: Jamie Miller, RN	Room: ED-6
Name: Avila, Timothy DOB: YR-4/1/8/ Date of Admission: YR-2/3/11	Diagnosis: upper respiratory infection	Time seen: 21:04
		Iso:
Allergies: N/A		

PMH: Mother reports 3-day fever 104F, fever, cough, runny nose, decreased urination, decreased oral intake. Increased respiration speed and wheezing began ~8:00 pm YR-2/3/11. No family history of heart disease, cancer, or diabetes. No past surgeries.

Previously seen 3/10/YR-2 w/same symptoms

Ca:	Cl-:
Mg:	Glu:
Ph:	K:
INR:	CO2:
PTT:	Hgb:
BUN:	Hct:
Na+:	Platelets:
	WBC:

Evaluation: Patient and mother arrive via ambulance. EMS personnel gave verbal report that patient seemed irritable, had fever, wheezing, and cough. Mother reports that patient had such symptoms for a few days. EMS medic reported that a nebulizer had been administered in the ambulance to patient. Medic provided me with written report at that time.

Mental Status:

- ☑ Alert and Oriented
- ☑ Verbally Responsive
- ☑ Responds to Pain
- ☑ Awake

Evaluation

Skin color is cool and pink. Listened to lungs and checked vital signs. Evaluation consistent with tachycardia and tachypnea. Temperature of 104F. Patient wheezing and coughing. No grunting or decreased breathing.

Diagnostics:

IV:

Due to change:____

Wounds/Incisions/Drains:

Pain/last pain med: Initial 21:15pm; see DB

Activity: See assessment DB

Meds: Liquid Tylenol Nebulizer

Vitals & Frequency: Initial; see assessment DB

T:	103.9					
P:	164					
R:	64					
BP:	125/76					

Exhibit 3

Nita City Hospital

Assessment Data Base

PATIENT: TIMOTHY AVILA

Date/Time (y/m/d)	Name	Progress Notes
YR-2/3/11 21:04	J. Miller	Vital Signs: HR=164, RR=64, BP=125/76; 104F fever; tachycardic, tachypneic
YR-2/3/11 21:08	C. Smith	Vital Signs: HR=164, RR=64, BP=125/76; 104F fever; tachycardic, tachypneic; symptoms consistent with URI; Tylenol and nebulizer ordered. Response positive but slow. Chest x-ray ordered
YR-2/3/11 21:17	J. Miller	Administered Tylenol and nebulizer treatment
YR-2/3/11 23:40	C. Smith	Chest x-ray not explanatory for infectious process. Impression: URI
YR-2/3/12 01:10	J. Miller	Vital Signs: HR=163, RR=64, BP=125/76; 103.1F fever; will continue to monitor
YR-2/3/12 02:14	C. Smith	Vital Signs: HR=164, RR=65, BP=125/76; 101.5F fever; will continue to monitor
YR-2/3/12 04:15	J. Miller	Vital Signs: HR=164, RR=64, BP=125/76; tachycardic, tachypneic Fever at 102.5F Complaining of neck pain. Doctor summoned
YR-2/3/12 04:30	C. Smith	Vital Signs: HR=164, RR=64, BP=125/76; tachycardic, tachypneic Eyes crossing, neck pain Order lumbar puncture, CBC STAT; ampicillin ordered; administered by J. Miller
YR-2/3/12 04:48	J. Miller	CBC, Lumbar puncture performed by C. Smith
YR-2/3/12 05:30	C. Smith	Lumbar puncture positive for bacterial meningitis, CBC: grossly abnormal white blood cell count, elevated C-reactive protein level

Exhibit 4

Nita City Hospital

Department of Radiology

2102 Colorado Ave., #439
Nita City, Nita 47817
819-555-2187
Fax 819-555-2188

NAME: Avila, Timmy (Age 2)
DOB: January 8, YR-4
EXAM: X Chest 2 Views
DATE: March 11, YR-2
TIME: 23:37
ATTENDING PHYSICIAN: Smith, Casey

HISTORY: fever, cough, respiratory distress

AP and lateral views of the chest

FINDINGS: the cardiothymic silhouette is normal. There is no evidence of effusion, focal airspace consolidation or pneumothorax. The upper airway is patent. There is mild gaseous distention of the upper abdomen.

IMPRESSION: Normal chest.

I certify that I personally reviewed this study and agree with the report.

Sydney Chen

Exhibit 5

Nita City Hospital

Department of Pathology

2102 Colorado Ave., #477
Nita City, Nita 47817
819-555-2195
Fax 819-555-2199

CLINICAL LABORATORIES

NAME: Avila, Timmy
DOB: January 8, YR-4
EXAM: Complete blood count
DATE: March 12, YR-2
TIME: Oral Report given to Dr. Smith at 05:23
ATTENDING PHYSICIAN: Smith, Casey

HISTORY: fever, cough, respiratory distress

Complete blood count ordered by Casey Smith.

FINDINGS: Streptococcus pneumoniae.

Unusually high number of white blood cells. No organisms seen.

Elevated C–reactive protein level

IMPRESSION: Findings consistent with bacterial meningitis. Antibiotics recommended: ampicillin and sulbactum.

I certify that I personally reviewed this study and agree with the report.

Lee Wallace

Exhibit 6

Nita City Hospital

Department of Pathology

2102 Colorado Ave., #477
Nita City, Nita 47817
819-555-2195
Fax 819-555-2199

CLINICAL LABORATORIES

NAME: Avila, Timmy
DOB: January 8, YR-4
EXAM: Lumbar Puncture
DATE: March 12, YR-2
TIME: Oral Report given to Dr. Smith at 05:27
ATTENDING PHYSICIAN: Smith, Casey

HISTORY: fever, cough, respiratory distress

Lumbar puncture performed by Casey Smith in patient's hospital room.

FINDINGS: Streptococcus pneumoniae.

Gram stain—gram positive cocci in pairs and chains
Many white blood cells
Glucose— 0.3
Turbid appearance
Elevated C–reactive protein level

IMPRESSION: Findings consistent with bacterial meningitis. Antibiotics recommended, ampicillin and sulbactum.

I certify that I personally reviewed this study and agree with the report.

Lee Wallace

Exhibit 7

Nita City Hospital

Audiology Department

2102 Colorado Ave., #522
Nita City, Nita 47817
819-555-2105

PATIENT: TIMOTHY AVILA

Test Date:
April 2, YR-2

Assessment By:
Shay Flannery

Pure Tone Audiometry:
Test results were consistent with the diagnosis of profound hearing loss.
Timmy showed no responses to tones presented at maximum output of the audiometer.

Tympanometry:
Normal middle ear pressure and mobility.

Otoacoustic Emissions:
Absent responses to all frequency regions tested.

Speech Reception Thresholds:
Timmy responded to speech at 105dB in his right and left ears.

Perception Skills:
Timmy did not respond to any loud sounds and did not complete a play task when the sound was made.
Timmy did not detect voice.
Timmy did not respond to speech or discriminate words based on sounds.
Timmy looked for visual cues to understand communication.

Comments:
Evaluation was conducted while Timmy wore hearing aids.
Timmy's profound hearing loss does not provide him adequate access to sounds for language development or learning.
It may, with consistent use, and visual support, help him to be aware of sound in his environment and how these sounds may differ from speech.
It will be critical for his development to have school and family communicate using a visually accessible system, such as sign language.

Exhibit 8

Nita City Hospital

Discharge Summary

2102 Colorado Ave.
Nita City, Nita 47817
819-555-2100
Fax 819-555-2101

Name: Timmy Avila
Age/Sex: 2 Year(s) Male
Date of Admission: 11–March–YR-2
Date of Discharge: 4–April–YR-2
Room/UNIT: 4159 PEDIATRICS
Attending Physician: Casey Smith
Consultants: NONE

FINAL DIAGNOSIS:
Bacterial meningitis
Profound hearing loss

HISTORY OF PRESENT ILLNESS:
Patient presented at emergency room on March 11, YR-2, at 9:00 p.m. with a several day history of:

104F
Decreased oral intake
Work of breathing
Wheezing
Decreased urination
Increase in heart rate

For more detailed history, see progress notes.

HOSPITAL COURSE:
Initially, Timmy was diagnosed with an upper respiratory infection and treated with a nebulizer and Tylenol. Condition appeared to improve. Lumbar puncture and CBC ordered confirming diagnosis of bacterial meningitis after onset of neck pain and crossing of eyes on March 12, YR-2.

Administered Ampicillin and Sulbactum to treat bacterial meningitis and treated for a three-week period. Patient discharged to follow up with primary care physician.

April 2, YR-2, hearing test diagnosed profound hearing loss. For detailed history, see audiology report.

CC—Mother asks that copies of all reports be sent to primary care provider, Dr. David Sullivan, at Sullivan Family (45 Benson Pike, Nita City, Nita).

Exhibit 9

Nita City Hospital

Progress Made Here

Children's Health Information—Meningitis

What is Meningitis?
Meningitis is an inflammation of the membranes that surround the brain and spinal cord.

What causes Meningitis?
Meningitis is usually caused by a bacterial or viral infection that invades the cerebral spinal fluid (CSF). The severity of a child's symptoms and prognosis depend on the specific organism that is causing the meningitis. Meningitis can occur in infants, children, and adults. Some bacteria and viruses are more common in certain age groups than others. Meningitis caused by a virus is more common and usually less severe. Bacterial meningitis is usually more severe and may produce long-term complications or death.

How is meningitis transmitted?
The organisms that cause meningitis usually colonize in a person's respiratory tract and may be transmitted by close contact with persons carrying the infection, or by touching infected object and subsequently touching the nose, mouth, or eyes. The organisms may also be transmitted through respiratory secretions from a sneeze, close conversation, or by touching infected matter. The infection usually starts in the respiratory tract and then moves to the bloodstream where it may reach the brain and spinal cord. The infection may cause a cold, sinus infection, or ear infection, and then travel through the sinuses into the brain and CSF, although this method of transmission is less common. A child may have no symptoms at all, but may carry the organism in his or her nose and throat.

What are the symptoms of meningitis?
The symptoms of meningitis vary depending on the organism that is causing the infection. However, each child may experience symptoms differently. For infants, symptoms include: irritability, fever, sleeping more than usual, poor feeding, high-pitched cry, arching back, inconsolable crying, bulging fontanelle (soft spot on infant's head), and a noticeably different temperament. For children older than one year, symptoms include: neck and/or back pain, headache, sleepiness, confusion, irritability, fever, refusing to eat, decreased level of consciousness, seizures, sensitivity to light, nausea, vomiting, and neck stiffness.

The symptoms of meningitis may surface several days after your child has had a cold and runny nose, or diarrhea and vomiting. The symptoms of meningitis may resemble other problems or medical conditions.

How is meningitis diagnosed?
In addition to a complete medical history and physical examination, diagnostic procedures for meningitis may include a lumbar puncture (otherwise known as a spinal tap), blood testing, or a computed tomography scan (also called a CT scan or CAT scan).

How is meningitis treated?
Treatment for meningitis is based on the child's age, the child's overall health, the child's medical history, the extent of the disease, the organism causing the infection, the child's tolerance for different medications, procedures and therapies, and expectations for the course of the disease.

Bacterial meningitis is most frequently treated with antibiotics. The earlier the antibiotics are administered, the better the child's outcome. Most children with viral meningitis recover on their own without treatment.

While the child is recovering from meningitis, other therapies may be initiated to improve healing and comfort and provide relief from symptoms. These may include bed rest, increased fluid intake, medications, supplemental oxygen, or mechanical ventilation.

How is meningitis prevented?
Several vaccines are currently available to prevent some of the bacterial organisms that can cause meningitis.

For questions, please consult your child's physician at Nita City Hospital.

Exhibit 10

Nita School for the Deaf

89755 Patterson Avenue
Nita City, Nita 47823
819-555-7489

Social History Report

Child: Timmy Avila
Date of Birth: January 8, YR-4
Parent/Legal Guardian: Shirley **Avila**
Address: 2215 Market Street,
Nita City, Nita

Date of Interview: February 27, YR-1
Prepared By: Catherine Riley

Introductory Information

Soon after Timmy was diagnosed with profound hearing loss at age two, his mother, Shirley Avila, determined that Nita School for the Deaf (NSD) offers a program that best supports Timmy's communication and academic development. Ms. Avila describes her son as smart, playful, and though sometimes shy, very outgoing. Ms. Avila expects NSD to provide Timmy with educational programming that enables him to reach his potential. This includes Timmy acquiring the necessary communication and academic skills to graduate from high school and prepare him to both enter and graduate college.

Biological Family Information

Timmy resides in Nita City with Ms. Avila. Since losing his hearing, Timmy has had no contact with his biological father. Ms. Avila is a single mother. She works an office job during the day and as a waitress a few nights per week.

Timmy and his mother use rudimentary sign language, pointing and gesturing in order to communicate with each other. Timmy is able to reply to some sign language using sign language. Timmy gives good eye contact. Timmy is also able to vocalize or imitate some words with understanding, such as "eat," "juice," "milk," "mom," etc. To make himself understood, will Timmy point, grab your hand, and take you with him to show you what he wants. In terms of assistive devices, the Avila family home is equipped with TV captioning and DVD videos that teach sign language.

Educational History

Timmy entered the Early Childhood Program here at the NSD when he was two years old, September 10, YR-2. Timmy initially attended NSD two days weekly. At age three, Timmy enrolled as a full-time student at NSD. Timmy continues to enjoy and benefit from his educational programming.

Ms. Avila expressed interest in her family participating in NSD's Shared Reading Program. She also expressed interest in NSD's Day of Advocating for your Deaf/Hard of Hearing Child Conference. At this time, she has not participated in these activities, citing work conflicts.

Evaluation

Timmy is currently in pre-kindergarten as part of NSD's Special Education program for Childhood Development. Timmy's classroom has a small teacher-to-student ratio. Information is presented visually, using sign language. In this learning environment, Timmy has opportunities to interact with his deaf and hard of hearing peers, as well as deaf adults who serve as role models for the deaf culture. Information is taught directly and at a slower pace of instruction, with frequent opportunities for repetition and hands-on activities. Timmy enjoys reading books and can point to pictures and comment on what he sees, though he benefits from having stories read to him multiple times.

Timmy also attends a daycare program after the day is finished at NSD. His mother reports that Timmy is experiencing some difficulty, since the daycare staff is not familiar with working with deaf children.

Timmy was fitted with binaural hearing aids shortly after he was discharged from Nita City Hospital on April 4, YR-2. He wears both hearing aids in school consistently.

Timmy demonstrates very poor communication skills in comparison to what we'd expect to see from his same age hearing peers. Timmy's teacher, Matthew Brody, is very concerned about Timmy's lack of progress with his language development. Specifically, Mr. Brody notes that Timmy's expressive skills are lacking. Timmy needs adults to provide language models and/or ask him questions in order for him to express his thoughts and ideas. Though Timmy is curious and eager to learn, he needs to see new information multiple times over before he fully integrates it into his own understanding. A listener to conversation with Timmy needs to fill in the gaps to fully understand what Timmy is saying. Timmy's vocabulary is limited to the routine topics of the day. Timmy isn't able to include the subject and verb when communicating about something. During the school day, Timmy tends to watch other children chat and interact. He does not join into their conversation.

Recommendations

Timmy should continue to receive speech and language services to improve his language skills. Timmy should continue to participate in sign language services in an effort to continue developing his expressive and receptive communication skills. Timmy's family should also participate in the available services for learning sign language. Additionally, his family is encouraged to gain access to informed parental support to help them understand his hearing loss, his communication, and how it might impact his academic functioning.

More specifically, we recommend that Timmy participate in:

- Activities that use signs and follow directives incorporating spatial vocabulary, action vocabulary, and basic linguistic vocabulary
- Modeled conversational turn-taking while playing with a peer during a structured activity to give him practice in communicative exchange
- Novel situations incorporating repetition strategies to help him retain information
- Instruction using visual phonics cues to highlight sound visually, providing Timmy more information about English print and improving speechreading abilities
- Activities that encourage Timmy to initiate mouth movements for spoken vocabulary and improve his ability to produce meaningful words

Timmy would benefit from:

- His family working collaboratively with NSD staff as well as other professionals involved with his education and overall development
- A center-based deaf education setting where he can access information visually
- Visual representations, such as hands-on activities, and group discussions in sign language
- A small student-to-instructional staff ratio
- Working with professionals fluent in sign language

Exhibit 11

Photo of Cochlear Implant

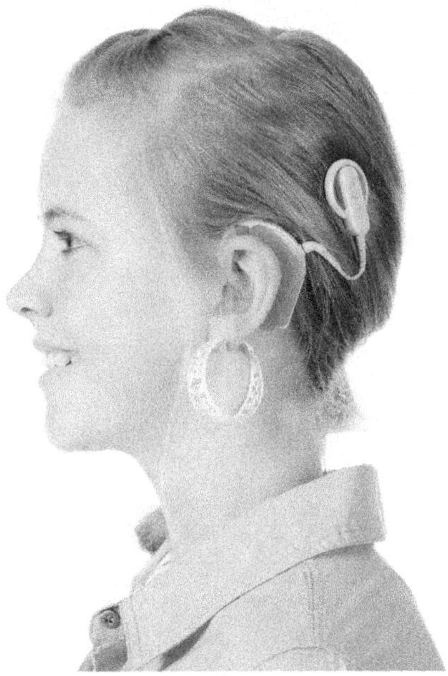

Exhibit 12

Facebook entry of Shirley Avila

Shirley Avila
March 9, YR-2 at 2:55pm ·

Timmy is sick again - it hurts me to see him like this. Hate to bring him to the hospital though. We bring him there too much!

Like · Comment · Share

4 people like this.

2 shares

Write a comment ...

Exhibit 13

Text from Shirley Avila to Timmy's Father

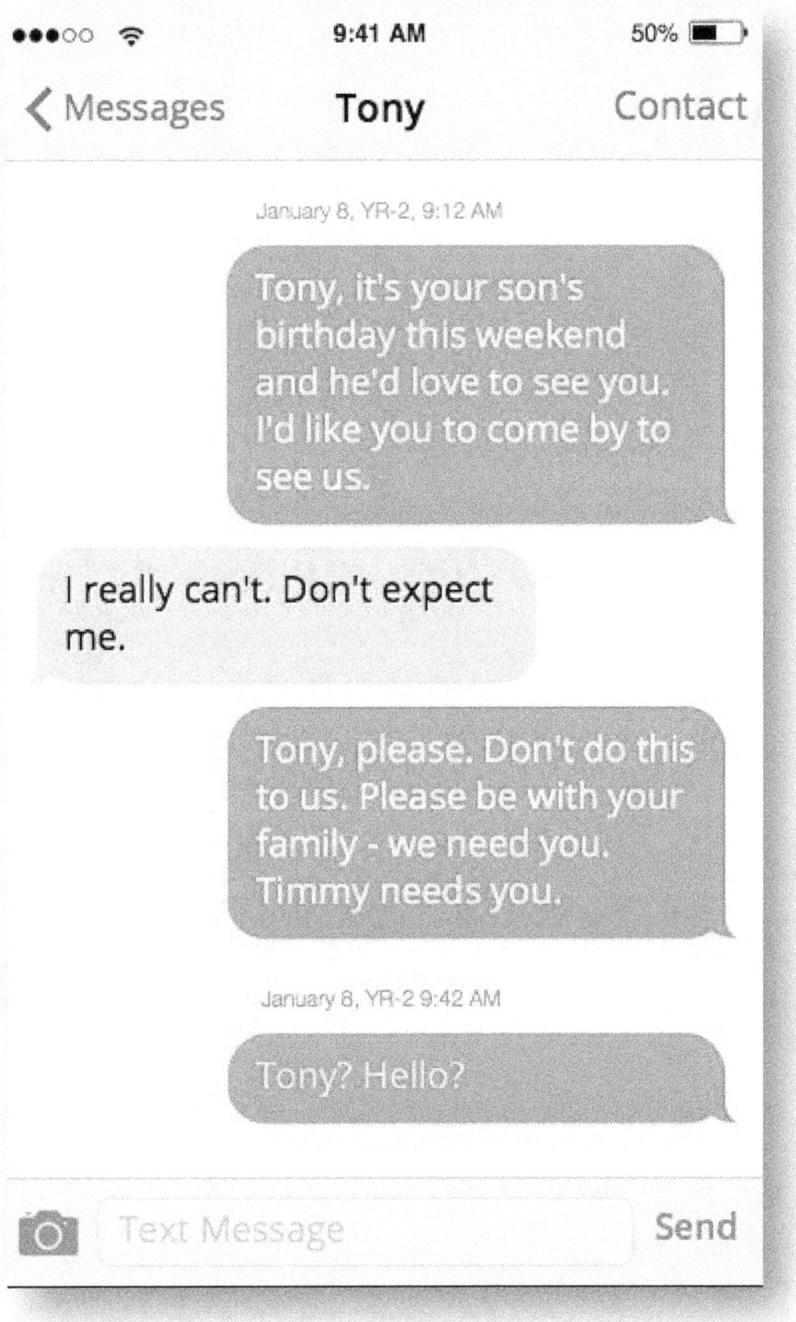

Exhibit 14

Twitter entry of Dr. Casey Smith

Dr. Casey Smith
@DrCSmith2143

Follow

Lethargy is often a sign of a more serious condition in the pediatric emergency medicine setting. Be vigilant for signs in patients.

9:48 AM - 11 June YR-1

Exhibit 15

Text from Jamie Miller to Dr. Casey Smith

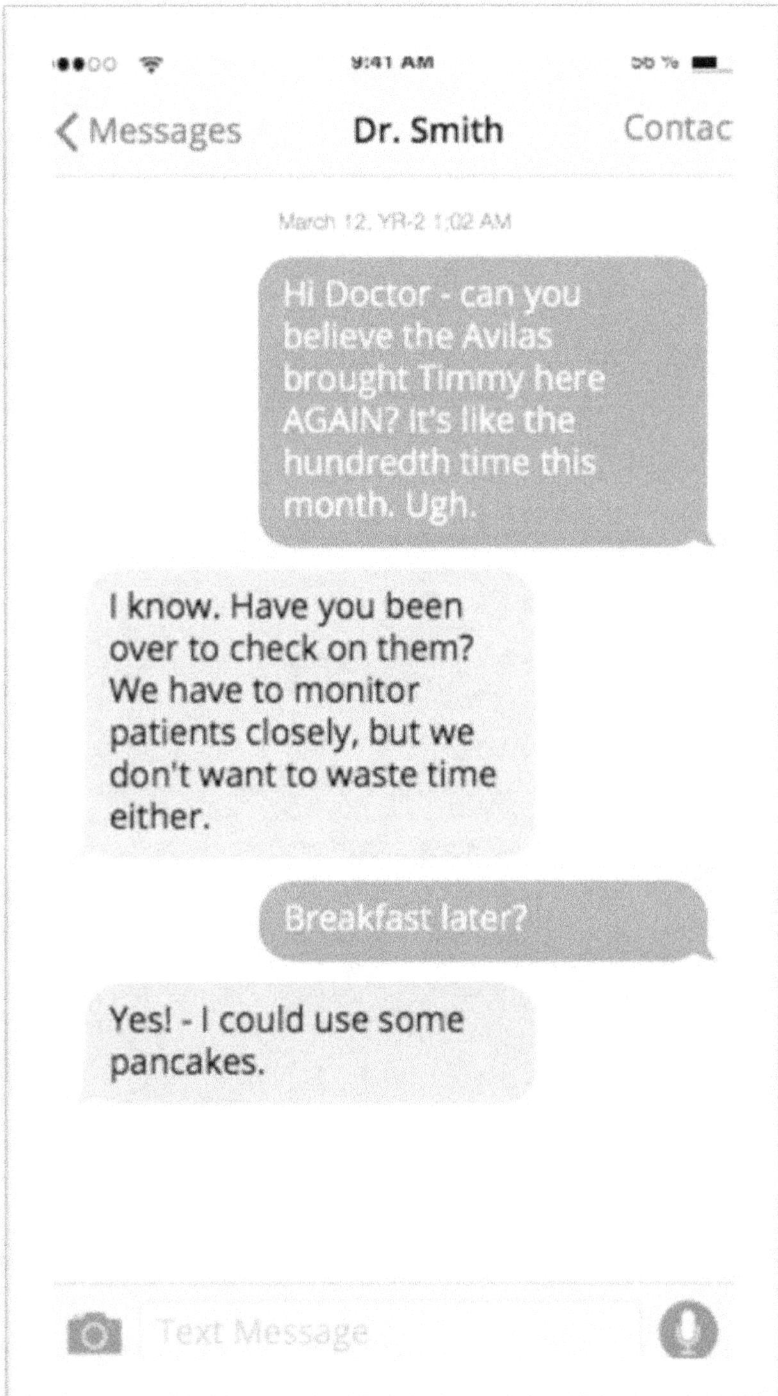

Expert Reports for the Plaintiff

Belleville Women's and Children's Hospital
76 Noel Lane
Belleville, Nita 47725
819-555-7878

Sam Simmons, MD, FAAP, FACEP, FACPE
Dep't Pediatric Emergency Medicine
September 15, YR-1

RE: Avila v. Nita City Hospital

Dear Plaintiff's Counsel:

Thank you for the opportunity to review this case. My expert opinions regarding pediatric emergency medicine will be provided in a nonbiased, objective manner, in compliance with the standards set forth by the American College of Emergency Physicians.

My opinions are based on, but not limited to, my education, training, and experience, as well as my thorough review of the following: Timmy Avila's medical records from Nita City Hospital (including progress notes, test results, and other relevant ED records), the EMS records from March 11, YR-2, and all depositions relevant to this lawsuit.

A brief factual history is as follows: Timmy Avila presented to the emergency department at the Nita City Hospital on March 11, YR-2. Timmy was ultimately diagnosed with bacterial meningitis. In my opinion, as a result of the delay in diagnosis and treatment secondary to substandard care, Timmy suffered permanent and significant neurologic injuries.

On March 11, YR-2, Timmy Avila presented to the ED at Nita City Hospital at approximately 9:00 p.m. with the following symptoms: a three-day history of 104F fever, cough, runny nose, reduced oral intake, reduced urinary output, irritability, decreased activity, and inconsolability. At the time of presentation, Timmy presented emergent increased work of breathing, tachycardia (155–160BPM), wheezing, and tachypnea (55 breaths/min initial). Timmy was evaluated around 9:00 p.m. on March 11 YR-2, first by the emergency department nurse (Jamie Miller) and then by Dr. Casey Smith. Their observations are documented in the progress notes that are a part of Timmy's medical records from Nita City Hospital. The progress notes reflect that upon presentation to the emergency department, Timmy had a fever, was tachycardic, and tachypneic. Such symptoms upon presentation are reflected in the EMS records as well. Specifically, the EMS records reflect that Timmy was having trouble breathing, was eating less, and was lethargic. When Timmy was evaluated throughout the night, and again at 4:15 a.m. and 4:30 a.m., by Nurse Miller and Dr. Smith, respectively, his vital signs remained much the same, but the fever had been reduced. These observations are also reflected in the progress notes. However, it is unsurprising that Timmy's fever had been reduced. Timmy had been administered Tylenol upon presentation. These signs and symptoms are also consistent with the medical literature on children's meningitis associated with Nita City Hospital itself (see "Children's Health Information—Meningitis"). Specifically, the hospital's medical literature cites "headache," "sleepiness," "irritability," "fever," and "refusing to eat" as symptoms consistent with meningitis in a child over the age of one. These signs were indisputably present in Timmy upon presentation on March 11, YR-2, and into the early hours of March 12, YR-2.

Timmy was diagnosed with a presumed upper respiratory infection. A chest x-ray was performed. However, when the chest x-ray was negative, thus not supporting the diagnosis of a respiratory condition, Dr. Smith did not order further testing or evaluation, contrary to the standard of care. Given the lack of a definitive diagnosis, in conjunction with the intermittent presence of what should have been recognized as lethargy, Timmy's clinical presentation was consistent with a severe bacterial infection process such as meningitis.

To a reasonable degree of medical certainty, discovery of a severe bacterial infection, either by immediate evaluation or by observation with admission and ongoing monitoring and further clinical evaluation, would have led to earlier antibiotic therapy and significantly improved Timmy's outcome. Antibiotic therapy would have, within reasonable medical certainty, significantly improved the outcome and prevented the development of permanent injury. Instead, the only "treatment" that Timmy received was Tylenol and a nebulizer. The fact that Timmy's condition while in the ED waxed and waned after the administration of the above medication is entirely consistent with a potentially severe bacterial infection.

Dr. Smith had the ultimate responsibility to address all of the substandard care that I have mentioned. The care and treatment provided to Timmy on March 11, YR-2 into the early hours of March 12, YR-2 was substandard in light of progressively worsening symptoms that were consistent with a severe bacterial infection. This significantly contributed to his permanent injuries and, at a minimum, increased his risk of harm. Timmy's mother reported the symptoms of Timmy's worsening state to Dr. Smith and hospital staff, and these reports were not addressed or explored by anyone at Nita Hospital. The potential for an adverse outcome should have been readily apparent to any pediatric practitioner working in an emergency department, whether specialized in pediatric emergency medicine or general pediatrics.

In the alternative, Dr. Smith could have consulted with an infectious disease physician in the emergency room in order to confirm his diagnosis. This is especially true considering the chest x-ray that Dr. Smith ordered was not explanatory for the infectious process. Dr. Smith did not do this, and that too was a deviation from the standard of care.

There were inexcusable delays in diagnosing and treating Timmy's bacterial meningitis. All of the tests that were ordered, including the basic diagnostic tests that were ordered and the lumbar puncture that led to the ultimate diagnosis, were ordered three hours too late. Despite the signs mentioned previously that should have suggested bacterial meningitis, a lumbar puncture was not administered until 4:30 a.m. on March 12, YR-2. This test should have been administered, at the latest, before 11:59 p.m. on March 11, YR-2. Had that test been administered, bacterial meningitis would have been diagnosed and antibiotics administered, severely decreasing the severity of Timmy's permanent damage.

I submit all of my opinions with a reasonable degree of medical certainty.

Sincerely,

Sam Simmons

Sam Simmons, MD, FAAP, FACEP, FACPE

Curriculum Vitae of Sam Simmons, MD, FAAP, FACEP, FACPE

Belleville Women's and Children's Hospital
76 Noel Lane, Belleville, Nita 57725
| Telephone: (819) 555-6425
| Email: Sam.Simmons@hotnet.nita

Education

University of Nita, Nita City, Nita, YR-41–YR-37, BS Biology
University of Delaware, Newark, Delaware, YR-36–YR-34, MS Physiology
University of Florida, Gainesville, Florida, YR-34–YR-30, MD
American College of Physician Executives, Tampa, Florida, YR-29–YR-11, CPE

Employment

Pediatric Private Practice, Port Neches, Texas, YR-27–YR-25
D&T Medical Services, YR-25–YR-16
Phy-National (Emergency Physician for DRMC), YR-20–YR-13
Josiah Healthcare (Emergency Physician for DRMC) YR-13–YR-12
Doherty Regional Medical Center, Director of Pediatric Emergency Medicine, YR-12–YR-10
Commonwealth Emergency Physicians (Emergency Physician for ILH), YR-10–YR-4
Belleville Women's and Children's Hospital (Pediatric Emergency Medicine) YR-4–present

Board Certifications

Pediatric Private Practice, Port Neches, Texas, YR-27–YR-25
D&T Medical Services, YR-25–YR-16
Phy-National (Emergency Physician for DRMC), YR-20–YR-13
Josiah Healthcare (Emergency Physician for DRMC) YR-13–YR-12
Doherty Regional Medical Center, Director of Pediatric Emergency Medicine, YR-12–YR-10
Commonwealth Emergency Physicians (Emergency Physician for ILH), YR-10–YR-4
Belleville Women's and Children's Hospital (Pediatric Emergency Medicine) YR-4–present

Awards

Richard T. Kast Award for Excellence in Disease Prevention Research, YR-30
"Safety Net Award" for Outstanding Research Project in a Public Hospital, YR-23
Special Commendation by the Nita Senate and House of Representatives for contributions to improving the care of children in Nita, YR-23
Special Recognition by the University of Nita College of Medicine for contributions to the field of emergency medicine, YR-20

Memberships

American Academy of Pediatrics
American College of Emergency Physicians
American College of Physician Executives Expertise/Lecture Topics

Previous expert testimony given

Hazzard v. Nita Memorial Hospital—Darrow County Common Pleas—Trial Testimony for Plaintiff—July YR-2
Rodriguez v. Loudon—Darrow County Common Pleas—Trial Testimony for Defendant—April YR-2
Estate of Chen v. Klein Cancer Center—Summit County Common Pleas—Trial Testimony for Plaintiff—February YR-4

Compensation

Research and Report Preparation: $250 per hour, plus expenses
Testimony at Deposition and/or Trial: $350 per hour, plus expenses

Washington University
School of Medicine in STL
660 S Homer Blvd.
St. Louis, MO 63110

Jody Holt
Department of Pediatrics—Infectious Disease

Plaintiff's Counsel:

This letter is a response to your request to render an opinion about Timmy Avila's care and treatment at the Nita City Hospital and my opinions relating to the delay in diagnosis of his bacterial infection and meningitis, as well as his poor outcome. I am retained by Ms. Avila's attorney. My compensation for this report, billed at $200 per hour, is $1600. Should I be called upon to testify, my rate is $325 per hour, plus expenses.

My opinions are based upon my education, training, and experience, as well as my review of Timmy's medical records from his March 11–March 12 visit to Nita City Hospital, the EMS records, the depositions of the nurse that cared for Timmy, the deposition of Timmy's attending physician, Dr. Smith, and the depositions of Timmy's mother and grandmother.

A brief factual background is that Timmy Avila presented to Nita City Hospital on March 11–March 12, YR-2, with progressively worsening symptoms. He was ultimately diagnosed in the early hours of March 12, YR-2, with bacterial meningitis, which cause permanent and profound hearing loss.

I am very concerned about the evaluation and treatment that Timmy received, because there was reason to believe that Timmy's condition was significantly more serious than an upper respiratory infection. Specifically, he had been persistently tachycardic (HR=164/min), tachypneic (RR= 66/min), febrile (~104F), and had become lethargic. This is documented in the EMS report for the March 11, YR-2, ambulance delivery to the ED. It is also documented in the progress notes from the emergency department on March 11 and March 12, YR-2. Timmy also had reduced intake, reduced urinary output, and abnormal respirations. Even without a belief that he was lethargic at that point, his presentation was very concerning for a significant infectious process that required further evaluation (blood tests, such as a complete blood count (CBC)). Such tests would have led to recognition of his bacterial infection and treatment consistent with standard of care, including antibiotic treatment, further diagnostic studies, and hospital admission.

It is reasonable, prudent, and consistent with the standard of care to have at the very least performed some basic laboratory studies (such as CBC). The hospital deviated from the standard of care when they did not perform any further tests to evaluate serious bacterial infection. Had this been done, the results would have yielded findings that would have appropriately led to antibiotic therapy and supportive treatment, based on the severity of Timmy's clinical presentation and illness.

In the presence of lethargy, along with other findings, a lumbar puncture should have been performed. The EMS records, verbally communicated to the emergency room nurse, were consistent with his mother's description of Timmy's condition as lethargic. However, even in the absence of lethargy, the other findings and history warranted a more complete evaluation than Timmy received. It is my opinion that consistent with the standard of care, Timmy should have at least undergone further testing and evaluation of his illness. The failure to do so was a departure from the standard of care. Had such testing been done, it would have led to a diagnosis of bacterial infection, allowing for proper treatment and reducing the likelihood of the permanent injury that Timmy suffered. Even without a formal diagnosis of bacterial meningitis, additional testing would have suggested that Timmy had a bacterial infection, which could have then been properly diagnosed and effectively treated with antibiotics. Had antibiotics been given earlier, Timmy would not have sustained permanent hearing loss.

It is my opinion that there was a significant delay from the time of Timmy's arrival by ambulance at approximately 9:00 p.m. until the time that the lumbar puncture was actually performed (over six hours). Such a delay constitutes substandard care and significantly contributed to permanent injuries and at a minimum increased the risk of permanent harm.

In summary, as referenced above, if Timmy had been appropriately evaluated, such an evaluation would likely have indicated bacterial infection, and he could have then been properly treated with antibiotics and observed. With reasonable medical certainty, the results would have yielded findings that would have promptly led to the effective administration of antibiotic therapy. Consultation with an infectious disease specialist would have led to appropriate treatment, which Timmy did not receive. It is my opinion that the failure to properly evaluate Timmy on March 11–March 12, YR-2, constitutes a deviation from the standard of care and substantially contributed to Timmy's serious and permanent injuries.

The aforementioned opinions are rendered within a reasonable degree of medical certainty.

Very truly yours,

Jody Holt

Jody Holt, MD

CURRICULUM VITAE

NAME: Jody Holt

ADDRESS: Department of Pediatrics—Infectious Disease
Washington University School of Medicine in St. Louis
660 S. Homer Blvd
St. Louis, MO 63110

EDUCATION:

YR-46–YR-43	University of Virginia AB Bacteriology (with honors)
YR-43–YR-39	Baylor College of Medicine Houston, Texas, MD
YR-39–YR-36	Baylor College of Medicine, Affiliated Hospitals, Houston, Texas, Pediatric Internship and Residency
YR-36–YR-34	Baylor College of Medicine and Texas Children's Hospital, Post-Doctoral Fellowship, Pediatric Infectious Disease

HOSPITAL APPOINTMENTS:

YR-10–present	Chief, Pediatric Infectious Diseases Washington University Medical Center, St. Louis, MO
YR-13–YR-11	Augusta University Health Infants and Children's Hospital of Georgia (Augusta) Director, Pediatric Infectious Diseases
YR-17–YR-11	Quincy Medical Center Houston, TX, Consulting Physician
YR-19–YR-17	Washington University Medical Center, St. Louis, MO, Associate Attending, Clinical Director, Pediatric Infectious Diseases
YR-29–YR-19	University Hospitals of Columbus, Active Staff
YR-33–YR-31	Nita City Hospital Medical Center, Nita City, Nita Physician-In-Charge, Pediatric Infectious Disease

LICENSURE AND BOARD CERTIFICATION:

YR-39–present	Texas State Board of Medical Examiners
YR-34–present	Missouri Board of Medical Examiners
YR-30–YR-18	Ohio State Medical Board
YR-33–present	American Board of Pediatrics
YR-23–YR-2	American Board of Pediatrics Subspecialty Board, Pediatric Infectious Diseases

PUBLICATIONS (not exhaustive):

Holt J: *Two cases of undiagnosed pediatric disease: a study*
Infect. Dis. 252:568–589, YR-32.

Holt J, Lynch J: *Treatment of childhood angiomatous diseases*
Am. J. Clin. Pathol. 87:466–473, YR-15.

Holt J, Green B: *Infections in Infants and Children*
J. Pediatr. 123:793–816, YR-14.

HONORS AND AWARDS:

YR-18	"Mark L. Reilly Pediatric Attending of the Year" Teaching Award Washington University Medical Center

PREVIOUS TESTIMONY (retained by plaintiff in all matters)

YR-3	*Blankenship v. Primary Care Associates*, Darrow County Court, Deposition Testimony
YR-3	*Quincy v. Nita Memorial Hospital*, Darrow County Court, Trial Testimony
YR-6	*Crosby v. Welby*, Darrow County Court, Trial Testimony

Ryan S. Donnelly
CRRN, Certified Rehabilitation Nurse
429 Martin Road
Nita City, Nita 57816
RSDonnelly@hotnet.nita

REPORT OF RYAN DONNELLY

INTRODUCTION TO THE LIFE CARE PLAN FOR TIMMY AVILA

Timmy Avila is a four-year-old little boy who was meeting his developmental milestones until March YR-2, when he sustained permanent sensorineural hearing loss secondary to a bacterial infection at two years old.

Plaintiff's counsel asked me to outline and assess the services Timmy Avila will require as a result of the unfortunate circumstances of his impairments. All of my opinions contained in this report with respect to costs are based on today's dollars, without regard for inflation, cost-of-living increases, or other economic considerations. Additionally, all of my opinions contained in this report are held to a reasonable degree of professional certainty.

MATERIALS REVIEWED

As a part of my analysis, I interviewed Timmy's mother, Shirley Avila. I also conducted an assessment of Timmy. Both the interview and the assessment were conducted in May of YR-1. I also reviewed nationally available statistics to determine Timmy's life expectancy. His life expectancy is seventy-six years. Additionally, I reviewed all of Timmy's medical records, which were provided to me by plaintiff's counsel (including progress notes, emergency department medical records, and test results), the EMS report, a report from the Nita School for the Deaf, and the depositions of Timmy's mother and grandmother, Dr. Smith, and Nurse Miller. I have testified as an expert witness before, almost always for the plaintiff.

MEDICAL HISTORY

Timmy was the product of a full-term, unremarkable gestation and a spontaneous vaginal delivery. Timmy was noted to be a happy baby and was meeting all of his developmental milestones.

Shirley Avila took her son Timmy, by ambulance, to the Nita City Hospital Emergency Department on March 11, YR-2. Timmy was initially diagnosed with an upper respiratory infection, but a lumbar puncture performed early the next day determined that Timmy had bacterial meningitis. As a result of this delay in diagnosis, Timmy sustained permanent sensorineural hearing loss.

Since that time, Timmy has exhibited profound hearing and communication deficits. He has difficulty keeping up with and engaging with other children his age on the playground. According to Timmy's mother, Timmy does not have any friends at school or outside of school.

Timmy's vocalizations are not intelligible. Timmy communicates through gestures and signs. Timmy's family has limited knowledge of sign language. Timmy often points to what he wants or takes his family members by the hand to show them. Timmy has to wear bilateral hearing aids to attempt to alert him to various types of warning signals. According to Timmy's mother, Timmy often removes the hearing aids, and, as a result, the devices often require repair and replacement parts.

Timmy currently attends Nita School for the Deaf. He is taught sign language and receives special education and group speech therapy.

EXPLANATION OF NEEDS

Timmy will require additional primary care visits, over and above routine health maintenance, for management of recurrent ear infections and excessive cerumen that interferes with his hearing aids. Timmy will likely require an annual average of three to five visits to primary and specialty physicians through age twenty-one. Thereafter, an average of two to four visits per year will be required for ongoing observation.

An annual evaluation by an otolaryngologist will be required to monitor the status and function of Timmy's hearing.

Timmy was also evaluated for cochlear implants and was noted to be an appropriate candidate. However, Timmy's mother has deferred this treatment due to potential risks of the surgery, such as recurrence of meningitis and facial paralysis. The option for Timmy to have this procedure in the future is one that needs to be periodically reevaluated. Cochlear implantation has associated with it the cost of surgery, the device, and postoperative rehabilitation. Such ongoing care must also include family training to manage the implant.

Alternate to the cochlear implants, Timmy will require specialized equipment to facilitate communication, such as an ear-level FM amplification system with ultra-power hearing aids, which must be replaced every three years. Frequently, Timmy's hearing aids will need to be checked, repaired, and furnished with replacement parts. Ear molds must be replaced at least annually, likely increasing in frequency as Timmy grows. Timmy may require the services of an interpreter to facilitate communication in a community setting.

Timmy will require a very specialized and intense program throughout his education. This will include tutors and speech therapists trained to work with the deaf and hard of hearing. I recommend four to six hours per week over the next two years, and then four to six hours per month thereafter until age twenty-one.

Timmy's mother has been affected by his deafness. She must cope with his frustration of not being able to communicate much of the time, as well as with her own concerns for his future. She finds that her attempts to learn sign language and other strategies to enhance Timmy's development challenging. The need for follow-up care with multiple health care providers also presents a major challenge to his mother, who lives in a one-parent household and works a full-time job and a part-time job. Additionally, Timmy will require attendant care and supervision. People who suffer from profound hearing loss need protection relating to things that we take for granted, such as the inability to hear critical warnings like a fire alarm. Timmy's mother would benefit from an average of two to four hours of assistance on weekdays and five to ten hours on weekends, to provide respite and to guarantee Timmy's safety. Once Timmy reaches age twenty-one, he will require five to ten hours of assistance per week to help with life skills.

	One-Time Cost	Annual Cost *(ages 5–12)*	Annual Cost *(ages 13–21)*	Annual Cost *(ages 22–life)* *Independent with Support*
Medical Surveillance	0	$812	$812	$609
Otolaryngologist / Audiologist	0	$575	$575	$575
Equipment / Supplies	0	$3,351	$3,351	$3,351
Case Management	0	$2,950	$2,950	$2,950
Therapeutic Modalities / Educational Supplementation	$48,100	$13,200	$13,200	$6,090
Total Annual Cost	$48,100	$20,888	$20,888	$13,575
Number of Years	once	8	9	54
Total Cost	$48,100	$167,104	$187,992	$733,050

TOTAL COSTS OF SERVICES REQUIRED

TOTAL = $1,136,246

SUMMARY

Timmy will never have a normal conversation, experience the simple pleasures of the sounds of birds singing, or enjoy listening to music. While most children become more independent with time, Timmy is likely to continue to require significant amounts of supervision and intervention. His employment and independent living options will likely be compromised by the handicap of deafness.

I state these findings with a reasonable degree of medical certainty. My fee for this report is $1,750.

Best Regards,

Ryan S. Donnelly

Ryan S. Donnelly

Ryan S. Donnelly

CRRN, Certified Rehabilitation Nurse
429 Martin Road
Nita City, Nita 57816
RSDonnelly@hotnet.nita

CURRICULUM VITAE

PROFESSIONAL EDUCATION

- Master of Science in Nursing (MSN), University of Maryland, Baltimore, YR-20
- Bachelor of Science in Nursing (BSN), University of Nita, Nita City, YR-32

NURSING LICENSURE

- Nita YR-24–present
- Maryland YR-32–present

CERTIFICATION

- Certified Rehabilitation Registered Nurse (CRRN)
- Certified Nurse Life Care Planner (CNLCP)
- Certified Life Care Planner (CLCP)

PROFESSIONAL AFFILIATIONS

- Association of Rehabilitation Nurses (ARN)
- American Association of Nurse Life Care Planners (AANLCP)
- International Association of Rehabilitation Professionals (IARP)

PROFESSIONAL EXPERIENCE

- YR-31–YR-27—American Rehabilitation Hospital, Staff Nurse
- YR-27–YR-24—Hamilton Hospital Center, Rehabilitation Nurse
- YR-23–YR-20—Nita Home Health Services, Home Care Speciality
- YR-20–YR-11—Robinson and Associates, Medical Legal Consulting
- YR-11–present—NitaCare Nursing Solutions, Life Care Planning and Case Management (both pediatric and adult)

PUBLICATIONS AND PRESENTATIONS

- *Life Care Planning and Nursing*, Third Edition, Nita Legal Publishing, YR-9
- Family Involvement in a Life Care Plan, Nita Legal Publishing, YR-8
- *Creating a Life Care Plan with Loss of Hearing* (Presentation), Mid-Atlantic Nursing Conference, YR-8

CONTINUING EDUCATION (a partial list)

- YR-9—Introduction to Case Management, Continuing Education for Case Managers
- YR-8—Achieving New Highs in Life Care Planning, Annual AANLCP Conference
- YR-7—Revolutionary Changes in Life Care Planning, American Rehabilitation Professionals Conference
- YR-6—Rehabilitation and Life Care Planning Summit YR-6, International Association of Rehabilitation Professionals

TESTIMONY IN PREVIOUS CASES (past 5 years)

- *Anderson v. Nita City*—YR-1, Darrow County Court of Common Pleas, Testified for Plaintiff
- *Maguire v. Dunn Medical*—YR-1, U.S. District Court, Testified for Plaintiff
- *Wood v. Michaelson*—YR-2, Darrow County Court of Common Pleas, Testified for Plaintiff
- *Ricci v. Hunter*—YR-3, Summit County Court of Common Pleas, Testified for Plaintiff
- *Castor v. Popov*—YR-4, Darrow County Court of Common Pleas, Testified for Defendant
- *Anastas v. Nita Memorial Hospital*—YR-5, Summit County Court of Common Pleas, Testified for Plaintiff

New Wave Actuarial—Economic Consulting

72 Bethany Road
Nita City, Nita 57818
Cameron T. Patrick, ASA, MAAA
Phone: (819) 555-4924 **Email: CTPatrick@newwave.nita**

Loss of Earning Capacity and Fringe Benefits Report for Timmy Avila

BACKGROUND

Timmy Avila was born on January 8, YR-4. It has been alleged that Timmy's hearing loss resulted from a failure to timely diagnose and treat bacterial meningitis during his emergency department visit that spanned March 11 and March 12, YR-2. Timmy will now require ongoing personal and medical care for the duration of his lifetime. Timmy lives at home with his mother, Shirley Avila. Shirley Avila is a high school graduate. She currently works an office job during the day and as a waitress a few nights per week.

LIFE EXPECTANCY

The normal life expectancy for a male of Timmy's age is an additional 72.9 years. As such, Timmy will likely live to the age of seventy-six.

WORKLIFE EXPECTANCY

This report considers an anticipated level of educational attainment for Timmy that would be equal to or greater than the educational level of his parents. Therefore, calculations are provided in this report based upon the average earnings levels with a high school diploma, an associate's degree, and a bachelor's degree. These calculations break down as follows:

- Based upon the completion of a high school diploma, entrance to the labor market would have been approximately age eighteen. Therefore, the future worklife expectancy period with a high school diploma would be forty-seven years, based upon work through retirement at age sixty-five.
- The expected date of entrance to the labor market with an associate's degree would have been approximately age twenty. Therefore, the future worklife expectancy period with an associate's degree would be forty-five years, based upon work through retirement at age sixty-five.
- The expected date of entrance to the labor market with a bachelor's degree would have been approximately age twenty-two. Therefore, the future worklife expectancy period with a bachelor's degree would be forty-three years, based upon work through retirement at age sixty-five.

Work through retirement at age sixty would be five years shorter. Work through retirement at seventy would be five years longer.

FUTURE LOST EARNING CAPACITY

Lost earning capacity is measured for the duration of the future worklife expectancy period, based upon the average level of earnings (by age groupings) for the three alternative levels of educational attainment described previously: a high school diploma, an associate's degree, and a bachelor's degree.

Lost earning capacity is calculated by making an allowance for future increases in earnings due to inflation and productivity. However, the future lost earning capacity must also be reduced to its present value at an appropriate rate of interest. By using rates of growth in earnings that are representative of average rates of growth in earnings in the U.S. labor market, and using interest rates that reflect current interest rates in the U.S. economy, the allowance for future growth in earnings coupled with the reduction of future earnings to their present value would be approximately equivalent to a reduction to present worth at 2.5 percent net interest for present value.

However, people with severe to profound hearing loss before retirement are expected to earn 50 percent to 70 percent less than their non-hearing-impaired peers. As such, it should be noted that the costs included in the summary section reflect 100 percent of normal total earnings.

FUTURE LOST FRINGE BENEFITS

It is appropriate to make a calculation for the value of lost fringe benefits in connection with the amount of lost earning capacity for Timmy. Such fringe benefits would include the value of employer contributions to Social Security, retirement plans, and other fringe benefits. The future lost fringe benefits are measured for the duration of the future worklife expectancy period, utilizing the net interest rate method as described previously.

SUMMARY OF TOTAL FOR THE FUTURE LOST EARNING CAPACITY AND THE FUTURE LOST FRINGE BENEFITS

Lost Wages

2.5% Net Interest	High School Diploma	Associate's Degree	Bachelor's Degree
Retirement at 60	$836,397	$986,456	$1,304,762
Retirement at 65	$903,434	$1,069,626	$1,420,507
Retirement at 70	$974,047	$1,127,701	$1,508,939

Fringe Benefits

2.5% Net Interest	High School Diploma	Associate's Degree	Bachelor's Degree
Retirement at 60	$167,279	$197,291	$318,210
Retirement at 65	$180,669	$213,925	$348,964
Retirement at 70	$194,809	$224,540	$378,527

According to Ryan Donnelly, the total cost of services that will be required throughout Timmy's life is $1,136,246. Thus, future lost earning capacity, future lost fringe benefits, and total cost of required services will range from $2,139,922 to $2,946,973, depending upon retirement age and degree attained.

The opinions I have stated are offered with a reasonable degree of professional certainty, based upon my training and experience and my review of the medical reports and the depositions taken for this case.

Very truly yours,

Cameron Patrick

Cameron T. Patrick, ASA, MAAA
New Wave Actuarial—Economic Consulting
72 Bethany Road
Nita City, Nita 57818
Phone: (819) 555-4924 ♦ Email: CTPatrick@newwave.nita

EDUCATION AND CERTIFICATION

March YR-17	Admitted as a Member of the **American Academy of Actuaries**
May YR-25	Admitted as Associate of the **Society of Actuaries** (ASA) upon completion of required examinations covering the topics of advanced mathematics, statistics, applied statistics, operations research, numerical analysis, interest theory, actuarial math, risk theory, and survival models.
August YR-26	Master of Science Degree, Actuarial Sciences, **Vanderbilt University**
May YR-34	Bachelor of Science Degree in Economics, **Wharton School of the University of Pennsylvania**. Dual Majors: Actuarial Science and Decision Sciences.

EMPLOYMENT

February YR-37–present	**New Wave Actuarial—Economic Consulting** — Providing services in the evaluation of claims that arise from wrongful death, injury, divorce, and similar matters, using actuarial methods. Admitted as expert witness for courtroom testimony.

ASSOCIATIONS

Society of Actuaries
Member of the American Academy of Actuaries
Actuaries Club of Nita
American Economics Association

ARTICLES

"Assessing the Financial Implications of Future Medical Expenses for Injured Children," Nita Legal Journal, 12/29/YR-25

TESTIMONIAL EXPERIENCE

Kowlacki v. Michron Tech, YR-2, Darrow County Court, for Plaintiff
Gryson v. Belden Brewing, LLC, YR-2, Summit Cty, Court, for Plaintiff
Lemuel v. Dixon, YR-4, Mason County, for Plaintiff, for Plaintiff
Adams v. Everett Shipping, LLC, YR-4, U.S. District Court, for Plaintiff

COMPENSATION RATE

Research, report preparation	$200/hour
In-person testimony	$325/hour + expenses

Expert Reports for the Defense

HOSPITAL FOR CHILDREN—BOSTON

2804 Beacon Knob Boulevard
Boston, MA 02131

617-555-7070
Fax: 617-555-7071

HCBoston.nita

LOGAN A. LEWIS, MD
Division Chief
Medical Director

October 7, YR-1

RE: Avila v. Nita City Hospital

Dear Defense Counsel:

Thank you for asking me to review this case. I am familiar with the professional standards of care required and the applicable facts and circumstances in this case. I have read the relevant documents and medical records pertaining to the care and treatment of Timmy Avila on March 11–12, YR-2. Those documents and records include: Timmy's medical records from his March 11 and March 12 visit to Nita City Hospital (progress notes, ED records, and all test results), the EMS records, the depositions of the nurse who cared for Timmy, the deposition of Timmy's attending physician, Dr. Smith, and the depositions of Timmy's mother and grandmother. I have also reviewed the expert reports prepared by the plaintiff.

It is my opinion that the treatment of Timmy, including the associated timing of the course of management, complied with the standard of care in a pediatric emergency department.

Dr. Simmons contends that there should have been a higher index of suspicion for a severe bacterial or viral infection that warranted further evaluation. Given the symptoms and examination findings localized to the respiratory system, a chest x-ray without further testing did comport with the standard of care. No further tests, including a complete blood count or a urinalysis, were necessary until 4:15 a.m. on March 12, YR-2, when Dr. Smith and hospital staff's progress notes indicate that Timmy's eyes had begun to cross. The standard of care for the evaluation of a young child with a fever includes taking patient's history and an examination searching for the source of the fever. Based on the clinical improvement that was noted during Timmy's stay in the emergency room—namely, a decrease in Timmy's fever—there was no reason to suspect a severe bacterial or viral infection.

Dr. Smith is criticized for the interval of time between Timmy's presentation at the emergency room to the time that the lumbar puncture was performed. According to the assessments made during Timmy's stay in the emergency department, there were no clinical indications for a lumbar puncture to be performed any earlier. Developing a list of possible diagnoses includes a careful assessment of the clinical appearance of the patient and the interpretation of pertinent laboratory and imaging tests. However, none of the hospital staff, trained to treat patients in the emergency department, noted that Timmy was lethargic. Lethargy is a symptom consistent with a bacterial infection—a symptom, though, that no one observed in Timmy from Nita City Hospital staff and was not noted in the progress notes. Timmy was listed as awake and alert.

Only Timmy's mother and grandmother, and the EMS report that relays observations from Timmy's mother, claim an observation of lethargy. Timmy's mother claims that her observations were ignored by hospital staff.

However, such a suggestion ignores the level of detail that hospital staff is required to keep when treating a patient. Dr. Smith and the nurse who treated Timmy made a plethora of observations of Timmy, and considered statements from family members in conjunction with their own clinical observations, and reported no signs of lethargy. The evidence supports that that was what was done here. There was no deviation in the standard of care with respect to history taking.

In summary, the care provided by the entire staff at Nita City Hospital, including the care provided by Dr. Smith, was consistent with the standard of care in pediatric emergency departments in the community. As emergency medicine physicians, we are trained to rely on information derived from history taking, physical examinations, and a patient's clinical course and response to therapies when administered. Based on the improvements that this patient exhibited while under the care of Dr. Smith, Timmy did not have historical or clinical findings consistent with meningitis or a serious bacterial infection up until the moment that a lumbar puncture was ordered. In fact, the presentation of this patient was one of an upper respiratory tract infection and bronchiolitis accompanied by fever. His improvement in vital signs and clinical appearance, as well as a lack of findings consistent with meningitis, did not merit a serious diagnosis. Simply put, Timmy did not fit the clinical picture of a patient with a serious bacterial infection.

I understand that Dr. Donnelly suggests that Dr. Smith should have consulted with a physician in the infectious disease department of the hospital. Based on the circumstances that were present up until the moment that blood work was ordered and the lumbar puncture was performed, there was nothing that should have prompted Dr. Smith to consult with another physician. Even if Dr. Smith did consult another physician, that physician would have been presented with the same signs and symptoms that were presented to Dr. Smith, which were entirely consistent with an upper respiratory infection. Put simply, it is unlikely that a physician in the infectious disease department would have reached a different conclusion, unfortunately.

I have reviewed the Nita City Hospital Children's Health Meningitis fact sheet, and all of the information contained within that sheet is accurate. However, the information contained in that document serves merely as guidelines. We expect medical professionals to use their own professional judgment based on their experience.

Based upon my education, training, and experience, and based upon the documents and records I have reviewed, I have formed opinions concerning the care and treatment rendered to Timmy Avila. It is my opinion that Dr. Smith and the nurse that cared for Timmy met the standard of care with respect to their treatment on March 11, YR-2, and March 12, YR-2, and did not increase the risk of harm. The opinions that I have formed are based upon a reasonable degree of medical certainty.

I enclose a bill for $2,100 for preparation of this report. If I am required to testify at deposition or trial, my hourly fee is $375.

Yours truly,

Logan A. Lewis

Logan A. Lewis
Professor of Pediatrics
University of Boston School of Medicine
Chief, Pediatric Emergency Medicine
Medical Director, Emergency Department
Hospital for Children— Boston

CURRICULUM VITAE

Name: Logan Anthony Lewis
Business: Medical Director, Emergency Department, Hospital for Children—Boston
Birth Date: May 15, YR-59
Birth Place: Queens, New York
Email: LALewis@HCBoston.nita

EDUCATION AND TRAINING

Undergraduate:

8/YR-41–5/8YR-37	Georgetown University	BS, YR-37

Graduate:

8/8YR-36–5/YR-32	Saint Louis School of Medicine	MD, YR-32

Postgraduate:

6/8YR-32–6/YR-31	Cardinal Scott Children's Medical Center (OH)	Intern in Pediatrics
7/YR-31–6/YR-29	Cardinal Scott Children's Medical Center (OH)	Resident in Pediatrics
7/YR-29–6/YR-27	Children's Hospital (MA)	Fellow in Pediatrics

CERTIFICATIONS

American Board of Pediatrics	Pediatrics	YR-28
American Board of Pediatrics	Pediatric Emergency Medicine	YR-25
Advanced Pediatric Life Support Instructor		YR-25–YR-17
Pediatric Advanced Life Support Provider		YR-17–present

LICENSURE

National Board of Medical Examiners	YR-32–YR-29
Ohio State Medical Board	YR-31–YR-29
Massachusetts Board of Licensure	YR-29–YR-16
State of Nita Board of Medicine	YR-17–present

MEMBERSHIPS in PROFESSIONAL and SCIENTIFIC SOCIETIES

Society for Pediatric Research	YR-19
American Academy of Pediatrics	YR-15
Academy of Master Educators, Boston University School of Medicine	YR-11

PUBLICATIONS (NOT EXHAUSTIVE)

"Current Management Strategies for Immediate Care in Pediatrics" (Clinical Pediatric Emergency Medicine, 5: 56–70)	YR-12
"Emergency Dept. Management of the Pediatric Patient with Tachycardia" (Pediatric Emergency Care, 23: 176–187)	YR-10

"Blunt abdominal trauma in children" YR-9
(Clinical Pediatric Emergency Medicine, 9: 33–42)

PREVIOUS TESTIMONY

Pike v. Nita City Hospital—YR-2—Darrow County Common Pleas Court—Testified for Defendant
Hoff v. Mason Medical Center—YR-3—Mason County Common Pleas Court—Testified for Defendant
Billson v. Mitchell—YR-4—Summit County Common Pleas Court—Testified for Defendant

Elliott S. Green

Pediatrics | Infectious Disease

PO BOX 7621 | Fort Smith, AR 72901 | Telephone: (479) 555-8085

Re: Avila v. Nita City Hospital

Dear Defense Counsel,

At your request, I send to you this opinion letter in connection with the care and treatment of Timmy Avila. I based my opinion on the relevant documents and medical records pertaining to the care and treatment of Timmy Avila on March 11–12, YR-2. Those documents and records include: Timmy's medical records from his March 11 and March 12 visit to Nita City Hospital, the EMS records, the audiology report from Nita City Hospital, the deposition of Nurse Miller, the deposition of Timmy's attending physician, Dr. Smith, the depositions of Timmy's mother and grandmother, and the expert reports prepared for the Avilas. To a reasonable degree of medical certainty, my opinions in this case are the following.

Standard of Care

Timmy Avila developed acute bacterial meningitis. His lasting injury caused by the meningitis is bilateral severe neurosensory hearing loss.

The care that Timmy received by Dr. Smith and Nurse Miller at the Nita City Hospital emergency department on March 11 and March 12, YR-2, met the standard of care. His presenting complaints were fever, cough, running nose, decreased activity, and increased work of breathing and wheezing. Admittedly, Timmy did have 104F fever and was breathing fast. He was thoroughly evaluated by both Nurse Miller and Dr. Smith, who obtained relevant historical information and performed comprehensive physical examinations. He was reassessed on multiple occasions. The multiple physical assessments did not demonstrate any clinical finding compatible with a serious bacterial infection until the point in time where Timmy's eyes began to cross. At that time, a lumbar puncture was immediately ordered, as well as bloodwork. Between the time that he arrived at Nita City Hospital to the time that the lumbar puncture was ordered, Timmy was nontoxic, active, and comfortable.

The working diagnosis of a viral upper respiratory infection was amply justified by the history, physical examination, and prolonged period of observation. However, the history of respiratory problems and the rapid respiratory rate appropriately led to the taking of a chest x-ray. The chest x-ray was normal.

It should be noted that for a child Timmy's age, nonspecific laboratory testing—such as a white blood count (WBC) and differential counts—cannot predict whether a child has a serious bacterial infection or meningitis. For example, even an elevated WBC or differential count would have been consistent with his viral infection. This would not have required further testing or the use of antibiotics.

Once the lumbar puncture had been performed and was seen to be abnormal, then antibiotics were rapidly and appropriately given. The management and treatment of this viral upper respiratory infection during Timmy's time at Nita City Hospital met the standard of care. There was little evidence to suggest, prior to the time that the lumbar puncture was ordered, that Timmy was suffering from clinical meningitis.

Causation

The biology of meningitis is often misunderstood. Whereas common childhood infections can produce fever, irritability, fussiness, and an alteration in normal behavior, clinical meningitis is recognized by a combination of fever with severely altered mental status or fever with some abnormal neurological finding, such as stiff neck, eye anomalies, asymmetrical neurological examination, or a seizure.

A viral infection, such as the one that likely caused Timmy's fever and increased work of breathing, can alter local resistance and allow bacteria to enter the bloodstream. In the vast majority of children, the bacteria will clear the bloodstream and meningitis will not occur. Developing meningitis in such a situation is rare. In such rare situations, antibiotics do not alter the risk of developing meningitis.

The effectiveness of antibiotics depends on the patient. In my experience, if the diagnosis of meningitis is preceded by a period of general and non-specific symptoms (e.g., fever, headache, aching, vomiting), antibiotics will likely not influence the outcome. It is only when antibiotics are withheld from patients with clinically apparent meningitis (e.g., seizures, paralysis, stiff neck) that such a delay in the administration of antibiotics lead to a worse outcome.

Clinical outcome in bacterial meningitis is not sensitive to the timing of antibiotics. Specifically as it relates to hearing loss, there is no relationship between the duration of illness before the administration of antibiotics and the risks of subsequent hearing loss. In the years preceding the events that gave rise to this lawsuit, the prevalent viewpoint was that the timing of antibiotics factored into the clinical outcome for the patient. Admittedly, at the time of Timmy's treatment, the idea of importance of timing in the administration of antibiotics and meningitis was the consensus in the medical community; clinical outcomes not being sensitive to the timing of antibiotic administration was not a prevalent idea.

Here, Timmy likely had a viral upper respiratory infection. Timmy developed clinical meningitis on the morning of March 12, YR-2, and was initially detectable at the time he developed crossed eyes.

Summary

The care that Timmy received on March 11 and March 12, YR-2, at Nita City Hospital met the standard of care. Timmy developed clinical meningitis in the early hours of March 12, YR-2. Even if Timmy had received antibiotics at an earlier time, the outcome of his infection would have been the same. Even if Timmy had been given antibiotics as soon as he arrived at the ED at Nita City Hospital on the evening of March 11, YR-2, he still would have developed meningitis, and he still would have sustained the same degree of hearing loss. Nothing that Dr. Smith or the nursing staff at Nita City Hospital did or allegedly failed to do increased the risk of harm to Timmy or could have prevented the meningitis or changed the outcome. None of Timmy's injuries are causally related to the treatment rendered by Dr. Smith or the personnel at Nita City Hospital.

Sincerely,

Elliott Green
Elliot S. Green

CURRICULUM VITAE

NAME	**ELLIOTT S. GREEN MD CM**
PROFESSIONAL ADDRESS	PO BOX 7621 Fort Smith, AR 72901 Telephone: (479) 555-8085
CURRENT POSITIONS	Consultant in Pediatric Infectious Disease Fort Smith, AR
UNDERGRADUATE EDUCATION	George Washington University–AB cum laude, YR-50
MEDICAL EDUCATION	University of Arkansas for Medical Science MD, YR-44–YR-40
ROTATING INTERNSHIP	Little Rock General Hospital, YR-40–YR-39
PEDIATRIC INTERNSHIP	University of Maryland Medical Center Baltimore, Maryland, YR-38–YR-36
FELLOWSHIP IN PEDIATR IC INFECTIOUS DISEASE	University of Maryland Medical Center The Children's Hospital Baltimore, Maryland, YR-37–YR-35

PRIOR POSITIONS

YR-15–YR-13

Senior Vice President
Consultant in Infectious Disease
Children's Hospital
Des Moines, IA

YR-24–YR-15

Clinical Professor of Pediatrics
University of Arkansas for Medical Science
Little Rock, AR

YR-26–YR-24

Director, Pediatric Critical Care Services
Krasner Center
San Jose, California

YR-35–YR-26

Attending Physician
Ambulatory Pediatric Clinic
Little Rock General Hospital

BOARD CERTIFICATION American Board of Pediatrics
Pediatric Critical Care (American Board of Pediatrics)
Pediatric Infectious Disease (American Board of Pediatrics)

PUBLICATIONS *Clinical Evaluation of an Infant*, Pediatr Infect Dis, YR-21; 11:454-468
Infectious Disease Emergencies, Dialogues in Pediatr, YR-13; 3: 743–759

HONORS AND AWARDS Selected, Doctor of the Year (YR-14)
Krasner Center Clinical Teaching Award Finalist (YR-13)
Attending Physician of the Year (YR-28)

PAST TESTIMONY *Mills v. Nationwide, LLC*—U.S District Court, YR-2, for Defendant
Haver v. Mason Medical Center—Mason County Court, YR-3, for Defendant
Johnson v. Nita City Hospital—Darrow County Court, YR-3, for Defendant
Colias v. Smith—Darrow County Court, YR-3, for Defendant
Harrow v. Grant Hill Hospital—Summit County Court, YR-4, for Defendant

COMPENSATION Preparation and research: $200 per hour, plus expenses
Deposition and Trial Testimony: $300 per hour, plus expenses

Biddle Rehab, Inc.

P.O. Box 8365
Boldenburg, Nita 57820
(819) 555-2222
Fax: (819) 555-2356
Email: ABiddle@BiddleRehab.nita

December 30, YR-1
Re: Timmy Avila

Dear Defense Counsel,

You requested that I review information related to the Timmy Avila—an almost four-year-old male with profound bilateral sensorineural hearing loss—in order to provide my opinions regarding future care and related costs outlined in the report submitted by Ryan Donnelly. In compensation for this work, I have billed you $1850. If I am required to testify at deposition or trial, my charge will be $300/hour, plus expenses.

I reviewed all of the information and records provided by your office, including the medical records of Timmy Avila, Nita City Hospital patient progress notes, EMS records, the depositions of all of the Nita City Hospital staff associated with this case, the deposition of Timmy's mother, Shirley Avila, and grandmother, Jules Avila, the report submitted by Ryan Donnelly, the audiology report from Nita City Hospital, and records from Timmy's school, as well as the reports prepared by experts hired by the plaintiff.

MEDICAL SUMMARY AND CURRENT MEDICAL STATUS

On March 11, YR-2, Timmy Avila was seen in the Emergency Department (ED) at Nita City Hospital. He was discharged home on April 4, YR-2, after an auditory evaluation indicated he had a bilateral sensorineural hearing loss.

Timmy is currently attending the Nita School for the Deaf, where he is communicating using American Sign Language (ASL). Timmy also receives speech and language therapy at school.

Based on my review of the records, Timmy is able to feed and dress himself. Timmy is mostly toilet trained with occasional accidents. Timmy's family and teachers describe Timmy as an engaging and pleasant child. Though Timmy's receptive and expressive communication skills are delayed, Timmy's non-language based cognitive skills are normal.

REVIEW OF LIFE CARE PLAN SUBMITTED BY PLAINTIFF'S REHAB EXPERT

Though I agree with some of the assessments made by Ryan Donnelly, Donnelly makes recommendations and includes costs that exceed Timmy's medical and rehabilitation needs. Ryan Donnelly assesses the cost of his needs at $1,136,246.

My calculations will be based on 71.2 years remaining life expectancy for comparison purposes. This figure is based on my examination of US Life Tables statistics and census information.

Medical Surveillance—It may be reasonable for Timmy to see his pediatrician more often during childhood years (five to twelve) for monitoring of recurring ear infections. However, Timmy does not require additional monitoring by the pediatrician from ages thirteen to twenty-one, or by any physicians into adulthood. As such, I would reduce costs associated with medical surveillance by $33,008.

Otolaryngologist—Costs listed are within reason.

Equipment/Supplies—While ear molds for hearing aids may require more frequent replacement during childhood, yearly replacement would not be expected to be needed through life expectancy. Considering a four-year replacement schedule, total costs for bilateral hearing aids would be reduced by $34,674.

Case Management—By the time he is an adult, Timmy is expected to be able to manage issues related to equipment replacement or scheduling appointments. Elimination of case management services during adult life would reduce total costs by $159,890.

Therapeutic Modalities—Timmy does not require tutoring based on his hearing loss. Hundreds of hours of tutoring and support is not appropriate or necessary. In addition, yearly provision of five hours per month of tutoring / behavioral support services is not required. Total costs should be reduced by $122,400.

Additionally, it would be highly unusual for an individual who is deaf to require any other sort of intense support, such an interpreter. Rather, it would be more likely that Timmy would engage in social, recreational, religious, or other such activities in settings where people communicate using sign language. Costs should be reduced by a total of $284,550.

CASE CONSIDERATION

Timmy Avila has profound bilateral sensorineural hearing loss. There are functional limitations associated with hearing loss and communication restrictions. It should be noted that many people who are deaf see themselves as a linguistic subculture, taking pride in being a member of the deaf community. Deaf people have organized many networks of social, religious, athletic, and other organizations.

There are not significant service or equipment needs directly associated with profound bilateral sensorineural hearing loss. Plaintiff's life care plan includes costs for hearing aids through life expectancy. It is typical, however, for those with profound hearing loss to stop wearing their hearing aids when they are teenagers or adults because the hearing aids do not substantially or specifically enhance communication skills. In the event that Timmy stops wearing his hearing aids, the annual costs associated with hearing aids (about $1,949 per year) would not be incurred.

Timmy has a physical impairment that dictates the need for follow up. Nevertheless, plaintiff's life care plan's recommendations and associated costs exceed what is or will be needed for Timmy.

COMPARISON of ASSESSMENT OF COSTS

	Donnelly	**Biddle**
Medical Surveillance	$46,690	$13,682
Equipment / Supplies	237,921	$203,247
Otolaryngologist / Audiologist	$40,825	$40,825
Case Management	$209,450	$49,600
Therapeutic Modalities / Educational Supplementation	$601,360	$478,960
TOTAL	$1,136,246	$786,314

Therefore, I would assess total costs of services required to be $786,314, considerably less than that contemplated by Ryan Donnelly.

SUMMARY AND CONCLUSIONS

Based on the information provided to date, it is my opinion to within a reasonable degree of professional certainty that the recommendations and costs listed in plaintiff's life care plan submitted by Ryan Donnelly significantly exceed Timmy's current or future needs.

Submitted by:

Andy Biddle

Andy Biddle
RN, MEd, LPC, CRC, CCM, CLCP, LNCC, D-ABVE, CNCLP
Rehabilitation Consultant

Andy E. Biddle

RN, MEd, LPC, CRC, CCM, CLCP, LNCC, CNLCP
Biddle Rehab, Inc.
P.O. Box 8365
Boldenburg, Nita 57820
(819)- 555-2222
FAX: (819)-555-2356
EMAIL: ABiddle@BiddleRehab.nita

EDUCATION

Bachelor of Arts (BA), YR-32, Social Welfare, Pennsylvania State University,

Masters of Degree/Education (MEd), YR-26, Rehabilitation Counseling, West Chester University

Diploma in Nursing, YR-19, Shadyside Hospital School of Nursing

PROFESSIONAL EXPERIENCE

Rehabilitation Consultant—Biddle Rehab. Inc. (YR-9–present)

Adjunct Professor—Pennsylvania State University (YR-13–present)

Supervisor of Case Management—Nita Vocational Rehabilitation (YR-16–YR-13)

Rehabilitation Counselor—Nita Office of Vocational Rehabilitation (YR-29–YR-16)

LICENSURE

Registered Nurse, State of Nita (since YR-19)

Licensed Professional Counselor, State of Nita (since YR-15)

CERTIFICATION

Certified Case Manager

Certified Life Care Planner

Certified Nurse Life Care Planner

Certified Rehabilitation Counselor

Legal Nurse Consultant Certified

PUBLICATIONS

"The Process of Life Care Planning" (Legal Life Care Planning, YR-16)

"Vocational Expert and Damages" (Life Care Journal, YR-14)

MEMBERSHIPS

Academy of Certified Case Managers

American Board of Vocational Experts

Case Management Society of American

National Rehabilitation Counseling Association

AWARDS

YR-15—Professional Achievement Award from the Nita Rehabilitation Association

YR-12—Cody Fritz Service Award from the American Association of Legal Nurse Consultants

TESTIMONIAL EXPERIENCE

Mather v. Cotton Health Systems	YR-2	Darrow County Court	Testified for Defendant
Johanssen v. Margen Paper Products	YR-3	Mason County Court	Testified for Defendant
Estate of Kikel v. Gates Industrial, Inc.	YR-3	Darrow County Court	Testified for Defendant
Price v. Vincente Market	YR-6	Darrow County Court	Testified for Defendant

McCondrey LLP
Financial Forensics &
Valuation Services
Group

30 North 11th Street, Suite 108
Nita City, Nita 57815
(819) 555-4510

Chase Myers—Principal

Re: Avila v. Nita City Hospital

Dear Defense Counsel:

This letter provides an economic analysis of Timmy Avila's lost earning capacity and life care costs. In preparing my analysis, I reviewed and utilized the depositions of Shirley Avila, Jules Avila, Dr. Casey Smith, and Nurse Jamie Miller; the relevant records from Timmy's visit to the emergency department at Nita City Hospital (including all test results, progress notes, and his medical chart); the EMS Reports; and records from the Nita School for the Deaf. I also reviewed the expert reports of Ryan Donnelly and Andy Biddle with respect to Timmy Avila's rehabilitation. Where applicable, I will make comparisons between my report and the report of Cameron Patrick, the economic analyst hired by the plaintiff.

The scope of this report is limited to a review and analysis of the alleged economic damages, if any, suffered by Timmy Avila, as a result of the alleged incident of medical negligence. Our report does not address liability, if any, and I am not qualified to render any opinions with respect to medical liability.

OVERVIEW

Timmy Avila was born on January 8, YR-4. Timmy presented to the emergency room on March 11 and March 12, YR-2. Timmy allegedly suffered a delay in diagnosis of meningitis, resulting in hearing loss. Timmy lives at home with his mother, Shirley Avila. Shirley Avila is a high school graduate. She currently works an office job during the day and as a waitress a few nights per week. She has never been married and has no other children. Timmy's father is not involved in Timmy's life and does not provide financial support.

Email: chase.myers@mccondrey.nita Direct phone: 819.555.4517

WORKLIFE EXPECTANCY

For the purpose of our analysis, we utilized U.S. Life Tables (2009), which indicate that the average statistical life expectancy for a white male at the age of four is seventy-two additional years.

Retirement Age

The estimated age at retirement of American males ranges from 61.6–62.6 years. Further, the median retirement age for American males is 62 years. The estimated age at retirement of men has steadily decreased from 67–69 years of age in 1950, to 61–63, where it sits now. Based on our independent research an expected retirement ages, I conservatively calculated alleged lost earnings using a retirement age of 62, three years less than the retirement age used in Cameron Patrick's report.

Mortality Factor

With each year of life, the probability of death increases. The truth is, there is not 100 percent probability of living until retirement age and that any person, including Timmy, could die from causes and/or events completely unrelated to the event that gave rise to the computation of lost earning capacity. For this reason, it is appropriate and proper to reflect the statistical probability of mortality from the date of measurement until the designated retirement age. This mortality factor should apply to reflect the risk of not achieving all future years of lost earning capacity for causes and events unrelated to the alleged incident. Interestingly, Cameron Patrick's report does not reference or mention mortality probability in future earning capacity.

WORKLIFE EARNINGS AND GROWTH FACTOR

Base Salary

Based on my review of materials provided, I have prepared earnings loss scenarios assuming Timmy has not incurred a reduction to his earning capacity (based on his ability to obtain levels of educational achievement beyond twelfth grade) and alternatively assuming he has incurred a reduction to his earning capacity (without consideration of education achievement).

In Scenario One, we assumed Timmy will obtain educational achievement beyond the twelfth grade, resulting in no reduction to his earning capacity.

In Scenario Two, we assumed Timmy has incurred a reduction to his earning capacity without consideration of the specific level of education he will achieve. Experts in my field expect people with severe hearing impairments to earn approximately 71 percent of those with no disability. As such, we determined a pre-injury earning capacity for Timmy at $32,688 annually. These are the median earnings for individuals with no disability. Timmy's post-injury earning capacity was determined based on the earnings for individuals with a severe hearing disability of $23,209 annually.

Growth Rate

The annual increase in wages and salaries for all workers is, on average, 2.5 percent. Further, we are of the opinion that a 2.5 percent future growth rate is appropriate.

Tax-free Fringe Benefits

Contrary to the assumptions made in Cameron Patrick's report, assuming future employment, fringe benefits such as health insurance coverage would not materially change pre- and post-incident. We applied a fringe benefit rate of 4.6 percent to the estimated lost earnings, representing retirement and savings benefits.

Present Value Interest Factor

Future damages for loss of earnings or earning capacity should be reduced to present value. There are a variety of issues to be considered in establishing the appropriate present value (such as risk of receipt of future lost income, term in years until retirement, risk captured elsewhere in damages model). For purposes of this analysis, we define risk in two principal concepts: probability of living to retirement age and time value of money. The first risk is captured in the application of a worklife expectancy that includes mortality factors. The second factor is predicated on the probability of receiving the future earnings for a specified number of years until the retirement age. I set the risk-free thirty-year U.S. Treasury rate at 3.7 percent, its most recent rate at the time of this report.

Future Medical Expenses

Due to Timmy's condition, future medical expenses are expected to be incurred. The estimated medical costs are based on Andy Biddle's rehabilitation report, and I adjusted for estimated increases in medical benefits and discounted the amounts back to the present value. For the purpose of calculating future medical expenses, we utilized the life expectancy of seventy-six, as previously discussed.

Medical Expense Growth Rate

I estimate that the annual growth rate for future medical expenses at 3 and 4 percent.

Present Value of Future Medical Expenses

Future damages for medical and other related expenses should be based on the present value of the future damages. After growing costs under each scenario by 3 and 4 percent, we then discounted the future medical expenses to present value using the most recent U.S. Treasury Bond yield at 3.7 percent.

SUMMARY OF FINDINGS

Based upon an analysis of the facts and circumstances, the earnings prospects, health prospects, and market forces, I have calculated the alleged economic damages for Timmy Avila.

Lost Earning Capacity

Educational achievement beyond twelfth grade..........$0
Without consideration of educational achievement..........$310,421

<u>*Future Medical Expenses*</u>

At 3.0 percent growth..........$365,746
At 4.0 percent growth..........$461,602

According to Andy Biddle, the total cost of services that will be required throughout Timmy's life is $786,314. Thus, future lost earning capacity, future lost fringe benefits, and total cost of required services will range from $1,152,060 to $1,558,337, depending upon the growth rate with respect to future medical expenses and degree attained. You can see how I got these ranges by adding Biddle's total to the lowest number possible and highest number possible contained in Myers. I did the same with the plaintiff's experts.

We appreciate the opportunity to work with you in this matter. Should you have any questions, feel free to contact me.

Very Truly Yours,

Chase Myers
Chase Myers

Chase Myers

Principal—Financial Forensics & Valuation Services
McCondrey LLP
30 North 11th Street, Suite 108
Nita City, Nita 57815
E-Mail: chase.myers@mccondrey.nita
Phone: (819) 555-4517

Summary of Experience

Chase Myers is a Principal of McCondrey LLP in the firm's Financial Forensics & Valuation Services Group. Myers is responsible for managing engagements in which McCondrey professionals provide, among other services, the following: value consulting; intangible asset appraisal; financial accounting impairment and other testing analysis; economic damage assessment; forensic & investigative accounting; and litigation support services. The client base includes individuals; private equity, venture capital and other investment funds; closely held companies; medium to large public and private corporations; government agencies; banks; attorneys; and accounting/consulting firms.

Experience

From YR-11 to YR-7, Myers was a Managing Director with ZIBC MHM, LLC; from YR-14 to YR-11, he was a Managing Director at SATW LLC, and from YR-17 to YR-11, he was the Founder and Managing Member of Myers-Dobbs Consulting LLC, a specialized financial advisory firm concentrating in business and intangible asset valuations; economic damage analyses; forensic accounting; litigation support; transaction advisory services; and, financial advisory and consulting. From YR-19 to YR-17, Myers was a Director in the Valuation practice at Chester Alfredson LLP, and from YR-20 to YR-19, Myers was a shareholder of Asset Assessments, Inc., a business valuation firm. Prior to Asset Assessments, Myers served as Vice President of Corporate Finance of a NASDAQ company and worked in the Valuation Services Group of Chester Alfredson in its New York office from YR-25 to YR-21.

Myers has qualified as an expert witness in, among other areas, business and intangible asset valuations, economic damages analyses, income and alimony calculations, finance, accounting, compensation, and other related matters.

Publications and Speeches

Myers is a frequent speaker and lecturer on accounting and finance, business and intangible asset valuations, merger and acquisition transaction issues, and family law related issues, including alimony/support and equitable distribution.

Education

BS—Finance and Marketing, University of Pennsylvania, YR-36
MBA—Accounting and Finance, The College of New Jersey, YR-35

Professional Licenses and Memberships

American Society of Appraisers (ASA)
Institute of Business Appraiser (IBA)
Association of Certified Fraud Examiners (CFE)
National Association of Forensic Economists (NAFE)
National Association of Certified Valuation Analysts (NACVA)

Previous Court Testimony

Winans v. Jaeger Enterprises—Darrow County Court of Common Pleas—testified for defendant—YR-1
Menory v. Byers—Sheffield County Court of Common Pleas—testified for plaintiff—YR-1
Hernandez v. Osceola, Inc.—Brighton County Court of Common Pleas—testified for defendant—YR-2
Lahey v. Lakeland Golf, Inc.—Darrow County Court of Common Pleas—testified for defendant—YR-3

Schedule of Compensation

Report research and preparation, $300/hour
Deposition testimony, $400/hour
Courtroom testimony, $450/hour

APPENDICES

JURY INSTRUCTIONS

Introduction (Read by the judge before the opening of plaintiff's case)

As the jurors in this case, you will be the judges of the facts, and you will be the only judges of the facts. You will decide what happened. I play no part in judging the facts. That is your responsibility.

My role is to be the judge of the law; that is to say, I make whatever legal decisions have to be made during the course of the trial, and I will explain to you the legal principles that must guide you in your decisions on the facts.

You are to judge the facts in this case based on the evidence presented to you—and based only on that evidence. The evidence will consist of the testimony of witnesses, the exhibits marked into evidence, and any material that is read to you. In deciding the facts of this case, you must not be swayed by bias or favor toward any party. Our system of law does not permit jurors to be governed by prejudice, or sympathy, or public opinion. You must carefully and impartially consider all of the evidence in the case; follow the law as stated by me in these instructions; and reach a just verdict, regardless of the consequences. It is your duty to consider the facts objectively. Your oath as jurors requires you to decide this case fairly and impartially, without sympathy, passion, bias, or prejudice, in accordance with the rules of law that I give you.

As the trier of fact, it will be your job to judge the believability of the witnesses. Size up the witness. Is the witness telling the truth? Does the witness know what he or she is talking about? How good is the witness's recollection? Is the witness accurate and correct in what he or she is saying? You may also consider the demeanor of the witness; that is, how is the witness behaving and responding to the questions asked? You may believe part of the witness's testimony and not believe other parts of it.

At the close of the entire case, I will explain to you the law that applies to this case. You must accept the law as I explain it to you and apply it to the facts as you find them to be based on the evidence.

Law (To be read after closing arguments)

Medical Professional Negligence

The legal term "negligence" is the absence of ordinary care that a reasonably prudent person would use in the circumstances presented here. Negligent conduct may consist either of an act or a failure to act when there is a duty to do so. In other words, negligence is the failure to do something that a reasonably careful person would do, or doing something that a reasonably careful person would not do, in light of all the surrounding circumstances established by the evidence in this case. It is for you to decide how a reasonably careful person would act in those circumstances.

Professional negligence consists of a negligent, careless, or unskilled performance by a physician of the duties imposed on him or her by the professional relationship with the patient. It is also negligence when a physician shows a lack of proper care and skill in the performance of a professional act.

Standard of Care for Medical Malpractice

A physician must have the same knowledge and skill, and use the same care, normally used in the medical profession. A physician whose conduct falls below this standard of care is negligent.

A physician who professes to be a specialist in a particular field of medicine must have the same knowledge and skill, and use the same care, as others in that same medical specialty. A specialist whose conduct does not meet this professional standard of care is negligent.

Under this standard of care, a physician must also keep informed of the contemporary developments in the medical profession [or their specialty] and must use current skills and knowledge. In other words, a physician must have up-to-date medical skills and knowledge, and if he or she fails to keep current or fails to use current knowledge in the medical treatment of the patient, the physician is negligent.

Causation

If you find the defendant is negligent, you then must consider whether the negligence was a factual cause of the harm suffered by Timmy Avila.

Under the law, we call conduct that causes harm a "factual cause." Negligent conduct is a factual cause of harm if the conduct played an actual, real role in harming the plaintiff. The connection between the conduct and the harm cannot be imaginary or insignificant. Causal negligence may be shown by proving that it is more likely than not that the negligence was a factual cause of the harm. There may be more than one factual cause of harm.

You can find a factual cause of harm even if a person's contribution to the harm was relatively minor or the result unusual. A person remains responsible for his or her conduct that causes harm, even if other causes contributed to the harm.

Increased Risk of Harm

When a defendant physician negligently fails to act or negligently delays in taking indicated diagnostic or therapeutic steps, and his or her negligence is a factual cause of injuries to the plaintiff, that negligent defendant physician is responsible for the injuries caused.

Where the plaintiff presents expert testimony that the failure to act or delay on the part of the defendant physician has increased the risk of harm to the plaintiff, this testimony, if found credible, provides a sufficient basis from which you may find that the negligence was a factual cause of the injuries sustained.

I previously explained to you that if you find the defendants negligent, you then must consider whether the negligence was a factual cause of the harm suffered by Timmy Avila.

If there has been any significant possibility of avoiding injuries and the defendant has destroyed that possibility, he or she may be liable to the plaintiff. It is rarely possible to demonstrate to an absolute certainty what would have happened under circumstances that the wrongdoer did not allow to come to pass.

Concurring Cause

There may be more than one factual cause of the harm suffered by the plaintiff. When negligent conduct of two or more persons contributes concurrently to an occurrence or incident, each of these persons is fully responsible for the harm suffered by the plaintiff, regardless of the relative extent to which each contributed to the harm. A cause is concurrent if it was operative at the moment of the incident and acted with another cause as a factual cause in bringing about the harm.

Agency

If you find that Casey Smith, MD to be liable, and/or any of the physicians and/or nurses who were involved in the care in question at Nita City Hospital, then your verdict will also be in favor of the plaintiff and against the defendant as well.

Expert Testimony

During the trial you have heard testimony from both *fact* witnesses and *expert* witnesses. To help jurors decide cases such as this one—involving scientific, technical, or other specialized knowledge beyond that possessed by a layperson—the law allows an expert witness with special education and experience to present *opinion* testimony. An expert witness gives his or her *opinion*, to a reasonable degree of professional certainty, based upon the assumption of certain facts. You do not have to accept an expert's opinion just because he or she is considered an expert in his or her field.

In resolving any conflict that may exist in the testimony of expert witnesses, you are entitled to weigh the opinion of one expert against that of another. In doing this, consider the relative qualifications and reliability of the expert witnesses, as well as the reasons for each opinion and the facts and other matters upon which it was based. In general, the opinion of an expert has value only when you accept the facts upon which it is based. If you find that an expert has provided an opinion which is based on a mere possibility, or which you believe is based on conjecture or speculation, I hereby instruct you not to consider this opinion in your deliberations.

[*Damages* (Read only if trial includes finding of damages)

If your verdict is in favor of the plaintiff, you must then find an amount of money damages you believe fairly and adequately compensates Timmy Avila for all the physical injuries and financial damages he has sustained as a result of the negligence you have found. The amount you award today must completely compensate Timmy Avila for all damages he sustained in the past as well as all damages you find that he will sustain in the future. Such damages include past medical expenses (to which the parties have stipulated), future medical expenses, future loss of earnings, lost earning capacity, and past and future noneconomic damages. You also must decide Timmy's life expectancy in coming to your calculation.

You must also address Timmy Avila's pain and suffering as a portion of your assessment. Damages for pain and suffering are compensatory for any pain, discomfort, fear, anxiety, and other mental and emotional distress suffered by Timmy. There is no definite standard or method of calculation to determine reasonable compensation for pain and suffering.

You heard evidence of the family's decision to decline the surgical implantation of a cochlear implant. You may consider that evidence as to whether or not that decision making should result in a reduction of plaintiff's damages. However, you are also free to disregard it

I am required by law to give you these instructions regarding damages; it is no way indicates I have an opinion about the liability of a party in this case.]

Summary

The Court did not, and does not by these instructions, offer any opinions as to what has or has not been proven in a case. Your oath as jurors requires you to decide this case fairly and impartially, without sympathy, passion, bias, or prejudice. You are to decide this case based solely on the evidence that you find believable and in accordance with the rules of law that I give you.

The plaintiff's burden in this case is a preponderance of the evidence. By this I mean that so long as you find that the scales tip, however slightly, in favor of plaintiff, they have met their burden of proof. If you find that the plaintiff has shown by a preponderance of the evidence that the defendant was negligent, the defendant's negligence was a factual cause in bringing about the harm/damages, and the extent of damages caused by the defendant's negligence, then you must find for the plaintiff. Plaintiff is not required to prove that it was the sole cause. If plaintiff has failed either one or both of these claims that I previously described, then you must find for the defendant.

IN THE UNITED STATES DISTRICT COURT
FOR THE EASTERN DISTRICT OF NITA

SHIRLEY AVILA, AS PARENT AND NATURAL GUARDIAN ON BEHALF OF HER MINOR SON, TIMOTHY AVILA,:	: : :	
Plaintiffs	: :	
	:	Case No. 17-108
v.	: :	
NITA CITY HOSPITAL, Defendant	: :	

JURY VERDICT FORM (LIABILITY)

Question 1:

Did Dr. Casey Smith, Jamie Miller, and/or any of the providers at Nita City Hospital fail to comply with the applicable standard of care? In other words, were any or all of the agent providers of the defendant Hospital negligent?

___________YES   ___________NO

If you answered "Yes," please go to Question 2. If you answered "No," the plaintiff cannot recover, and you should not answer any further questions and return to the courtroom.

Question 2:

As to any or all of the agent providers that you have found negligent, was that negligence a factual cause of any harm to Timothy Avila?

___________YES   ___________NO

Date: ____________________________

____

FOREPERSON

IN THE UNITED STATES DISTRICT COURT
FOR THE EASTERN DISTRICT OF NITA

SHIRLEY AVILA, AS PARENT AND NATURAL GUARDIAN ON BEHALF OF HER MINOR SON, TIMOTHY AVILA, Plaintiffs v. NITA CITY HOSPITAL, Defendant	: : : : : : : : : : :	Case No. 17-108

JURY VERDICT FORM (LIABILITY AND DAMAGES)

Question 1:

Did Dr. Casey Smith, Jamie Miller, and/or any of the providers at Nita City Hospital fail to comply with the applicable standard of care? In other words, were any or all of the agent providers of the defendant Hospital negligent?

___________YES   ___________NO

If you answered "Yes," please go to Question 2. If you answered "No," the plaintiff cannot recover, and you should not answer any further questions and return to the courtroom.

Question 2:

As to any or all of the agent providers that you have found negligent, was that negligence a factual cause of any harm to Timothy Avila?

___________YES   ___________NO

If you answered "Yes," please go to Question 3. If you answered "No," the plaintiff cannot recover and you should not answer further questions and return to the courtroom.

Question 3:

Please state the full amount of damages that you find for Timothy Avila as follows:

Timothy Avila's future loss of earnings and earning capacity

$______________________________

Timothy Avila's past and future pain and suffering, embarrassment and humiliation, disfigurement and loss of enjoyment of life and life's pleasures

$______________________________

Timothy Avila's future medical and other related expenses

$______________________________

Date: ______________________________

____
FOREPERSON

www.ingramcontent.com/pod-product-compliance
Lightning Source LLC
LaVergne TN
LVHW082347200926
848481LV00012B/3483